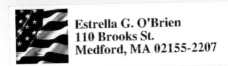

THE DARKEST CHAPTER

THE DARKEST CHAPTER

DAVID BEN-DOR

CANONGATE

First published in Great Britain
in 1996 by Canongate Books Ltd,
14 High Street, Edinburgh EH1 1TE

British Library Cataloguing in Publication Data

A catalogue record for this book is available on
request from the British Library

ISBN 0 86241 606 X

Typeset by Palimpsest Book Production Limited,
Polmont, Stirlingshire
Printed and bound in Great Britain by
The Cromwell Press

To my wife Edna – who stood by me,
To my daughter Nili – who wanted to know,
and
To the memory of
Primo Levi
who told the truth.

'Preferably the worst survived, the selfish, the violent, the insensitive, the collaborators of the 'gray zone', the spies. It was not a certain rule (there were none, nor are there certain rules in human matters), but it was nevertheless a rule.

I felt innocent, yes, but enrolled among the saved and therefore in permanent search of a justification in my own eyes and those of others. The worst survived, that is, the fittest; the best all died.'

Primo Levi, *The Drowned and the Saved*

CONTENTS

IT WAS NO 'HOLOCAUST'

In July 1989, the District Court of Beersheva sentenced the murderer of a Jewish woman. According to its verdict, her 'only sin was being Jewish'.[1]

There must be something terribly wrong with Jewish historiography, if while speaking about the murder of a woman whose very Jewishness was the cause of her being murdered, Jewish judges express that ancient Christian assumption that being Jewish constitutes a sin in itself. 'A figure of speech' some might say, but the fact that such figures of speech still linger in the minds of many Jews shows that the 'holocaust' has not changed their way of thinking.

Because it was no 'holocaust'. The term was coined by Elie Wiesel who stated: 'I used it [the word 'holocaust'] because I had no other word.'[2] I say coined, because Webster's dictionary defines the word as 'a burnt sacrifice: a sacrificial offering wholly consumed by fire'. (*The Concise Oxford Dictionary* carries a similar definition.) No sacrifice whatsoever was made or was intended by anyone involved, and the substitution of the definition 'murder' by the generalization, 'holocaust', has turned the destruction of the Jews of Europe from a definite political action – planned and executed by a sovereign nation – into some unfathomable scourge brought upon the Jews by supranatural forces.

By its generality, the hardly understood euphemism excludes any personal identification or involvement and frees participants and witnesses alike from taking any stand or action. As for guilt, even Germans refer to that part of their history as '*Der Holocaust*'. It exonerates them.

Yet it was the Jews who first willfully adopted the euphemism. Even before the popularization of the English word, the Hebrew term '*Shoa*' was introduced and used in every instance where Armenians, Kurds, Afghans or Cambodians would have referred to mass murder or genocide. In the same manner, the term 'Nazi' was introduced wherever 'German' would have been appropriate in order to bridge the obstacle of accepting reparations for irreparable crimes and to obliterate the guilt of the criminal and his helpers. One can obviously not accept reparations from the Germans and continue to brand them as murderers.

The terms '*Shoa*' and 'holocaust' came in handy to shield and exonerate those whose collaboration with the Germans assured to a very large extent the success of the destruction of the European Jews. Legislation in the State of Israel has always avoided the use of the words 'Germans' and 'Genocide'. Instead, pointedly and consistently, the terms 'Nazi' and '*Shoa*' are employed.[3]

Perhaps the wish to differentiate between 'good' Germans and other ones, has led even renowned historians, such as Martin Gilbert, to indiscriminately employ the word 'holocaust',[4] or Isaiah Trunk to use 'Nazi'[5] where 'German' would have been in order. What escapes beneficiaries and apologists alike is that although not all the Germans were Nazis, all the Nazis were Germans.

So now we have a new generation of teachers and intellectuals, writers and legislators, all Jews, who wish to forget and to obliterate the past – to disassociate themselves from it lest it become a warning for the future. They have completed the cycle by reciting, *ad nauseam*, on official occasions and memorial functions, platitudes bewailing the sufferings of the 'holocaust' and returned to the acceptance by Jewish judges, in the Jewish State, that 'being Jewish' can be a person's only sin.

And the one gap which still remains to be filled is the true answer to the ever-recurring question: How did it happen? What part did the Jews themselves play in their own destruction?

When Hanna Arendt proves 'the banality of evil'[6] or Raul Hilberg describes the historical process of a political action being conceived, put into operation and brought to a logical conclusion, I cannot help but integrate my experiences and observations – after years of introspection – into the explanation of that process by showing how, in the microcosm of my family, the road from a respectable bourgeois existence to collaboration was viewed as a normal development, accepted by its members as 'fate', not knowing at the time that this fate was shaped by what Raul Hilberg terms 'the interaction of perpetrators and victims'.[7] Hanna Arendt writes that 'to a Jew, this role of the Jewish leaders in the destruction of their own people is undoubtedly the darkest chapter of the whole dark story'.[8]

Therefore, there can be no 'holocaust' which absolves, obliterates, exonerates and relegates the most pertinent facts to oblivion. One's sufferings in themselves will not contribute much to filling the gap in the historical rendering of the destruction – nor do they justify the distortion of those fatal causes of which the destruction was the logical effect. They may serve as a warning to those who, by disregarding their past, could find it in their future.

3

CHILDHOOD

In the days when I was fresh out of Dachau, people used to ask me how I had managed to survive and what had happened to my family. I would answer that my mother and my brother were gassed and burned and that my father died of hunger.

In those years, nobody wanted details. Of course, everyone liked stories of atrocities, but the uneasiness shown by all questioners – their obvious discomfort – makes me regret, in retrospect, that the word 'holocaust' had not yet been coined. It would have been much easier on my interlocutors had I been able to relieve their embarrassment by saying that they all perished in the 'holocaust', especially in the days when the government of Israel began accepting reparations from the Germans. The satisfaction of the press and of most Jewish politicians was so great that, at times, I wondered whether my mother would have volunteered for Auschwitz had she known that the Jewish State would get money for it.

It was then that the Hebrew word 'Shoa' (the idiomatic equivalent of 'holocaust') became current, and all my efforts to convey my experiences were thwarted. The discussion would usually end with the unspoken implication that if you were there and survived, you must be mentally unbalanced. If on the other hand you were not there, then you don't know what you are talking about. The repeated encounters with doubt, disbelief or feigned pity made me gradually refrain from mentioning my past –

especially at job interviews, with friends and colleagues – lest the generally accepted notion of the mental imbalance of 'holocaust' survivors turned their judgments against me.

At times, I exaggerated the stories of my sufferings in order to emphasize the tragedy and to prevent my listeners from going deeper into the matter of how I really survived. Eventually, I withdrew the subject entirely from my conversations. My standard answer of 'pure luck' was not enough and gave rise to suspicions, which although not expressed, I knew to be well-founded.

My marriage and the birth of my first daughter provided me with the justification to change my name. I came to realize that it was my German-sounding name which always triggered an investigation. Are you from Germany? Where were you during the war? How did you survive? I needed a new identity.

David Ben-Dor. David was in memory of my mother's father according to Jewish custom. Ben-Dor means 'son of the generation of extermination and rebirth'. Changing my name was a *tour de force*. It was destined to suppress the past together with my identity. However, as in the famous joke in which a man changes his name twice to avoid being obliged to disclose his real name, my effort failed.

My employer pointedly observed that only a man who goes bankrupt changes his name. And just as bankruptcy is not revoked by a change of name, so my identity was not changed by it – nor was my innermost conviction that being of German origin with an awe-inspiring German name, I was still a 'Westjude', superior to anybody who could not speak the German language.

My decision to speak only Hebrew, as I explained to

my wife, was to give our children solid roots in Judaism. But it was also another brick in the wall behind which I could hide the past. I did not use the German language any more, for fear of giving myself away by relapsing into concentration-camp jargon.

As I am writing this, the English language protects me from reverting into what really is my native tongue, in which I still wish I could start each day's writing with the command shouted at myself as if I were someone else – a German: 'Los! Auf geht's! Vordermann! Seitenrichtung! Im Gleichschritt – 'arsch! (Forward march!)'

I became a proud Jew, disguising the long-felt inferiority of being Jewish and the hidden sense of superiority under a proud and modern Hebrew name in the same way that the Germans hid their inadequacies during my formative years under uniforms representing might and, consequently, right. But the questions never ceased; neither the ones asked by others nor those asked by myself.

Then, thirty years after I had been sitting on the grass, outside the concentration camp, wearing a discarded SS officer's jacket from which the insignia had been removed, watching American soldiers marching German prisoners down the road, pitying them because 'we' had lost the war – my youngest daughter asked the questions. And so, after three decades of hostile silence, answers had to be given.

It was not easy being interrogated by my own daughter. She had chosen the subject, 'The Destruction of the Kovno Ghetto: *Shoa* or Crime by Omission?' as the history project required to complete her final high school examinations. In her research, she had perused Garfunkel's *The Destruction of Kovno's Jewry*[9] for documentation and found my father's name on page 54. Of course, she wanted all the details. What had he done in order to be allowed to remain a whole year outside the Ghetto while the others were being led to their deaths? What had I done?

I can only attribute my carefully repressed, disguised, yet latent wish to become an SS man – wearing skull and cross-bones, to intimidate and rule – to the unassuaged thirst for vengeance against my father.

Dr med. Moses Haber, general practitioner, Defreggerstrasse 4, Innsbruck, Tirol, Austria (as his stationery proudly stated), hit my mother. Her maiden name, before she had married him in 1924, was Selda-Lea Weiner. Not having learned how to speak proper German was one of her 'crimes'. She had never mastered the proper German pronunciation of the umlaut, a 'crime', because back in Vienna, in his student days, my father had lodged with her family and had paid his rent by giving Selda German lessons. No matter how many times he corrected and humiliated her, she never learned how to pronounce those German vowels, whose improper pronunciation was a disclosure of her Eastern Jewish origin.

It was as if the well-to-do Herr Doktor resented the fact that she had provided the financial means by which he could establish his medical practice. Despite being of 'lower' social origin in his eyes, in her position as purchase manager at the town's only department store, she earned much more than he did. He did not differ from many German Jews who had acquired a higher education and who considered Jews from Eastern European regions as being inferior. They displayed this superiority for the same reason that their German neighbours wore their uniforms – as a mark of power and superiority.

She would smile when he tried to make her repeat after him the German umlaut, but that was not why he hit her. It may have been that the ingurgitation of German 'culture' brought out a dormant streak of brutality in him which manifested itself as early as my memory reaches back into my childhood. Constantly scowling, shouting, screaming at the top of his voice and banging doors – he was a force I had come to fear.

It was 1931, and I was three years old. I faintly recall a small dog who used to run from one room to another. One day he disappeared. For days I looked for the little animal, but he was gone. He had torn a tassel off a curtain, so he had to be 'liquidated'.

My brother was born around that time. They had named me Ernst David, but buried the second name – the one my mother had given me – somewhere in the community registry, never to be used again. They called the baby Hans. Ernst and Hans, the future Germans – or as we were then to become, 'Austrian citizens of the faith of Moses'. We grew up in an eight-room apartment whose carpets, paintings and sculptures were to assure our future, our security and our well-being.

The baby, whose bad smell rose from the carriage, became the only focus of my mother's attention. Having been born prematurely after a seven-month pregnancy, he now completely took her away. I was alone for hours and days, except for the times when our maid, Amalia, would take me for walks to the centre of town as a special treat. There her brother, wearing a splendid policeman's uniform, stood high up on a platform, right in the middle of the intersection, directing traffic. Up went his arm and everyone stopped. He was even more powerful than my father.

I changed camps. The more my father called my mother names, the closer I felt to him. It was my revenge on my mother leaving me. As the baby grew into a boy, so grew my hatred for him, for my mother, and for everyone else. Although I had chosen my father to be my ally, emulating and admiring him, I never stopped hating him – particularly because of what had happened on the 'Seder' night (the first night of Passover) in 1934. My mother had forgotten to put the salt on the table, so he hit her. I started crying and the memory keeps the tears returning to this very day – whenever my wife lights the candles; whenever I make the 'Kiddush' (ceremonial blessing over wine recited on the Sabbath and holy days).

SCHOOLDAYS

The fear of God was inculcated in me starting at the age of five. A teacher was engaged to give me Hebrew and Bible lessons, and he started with the order of the sacrifices in Leviticus. Having been repeatedly reprimanded for not being able to understand the purpose of 'a sweet savour unto the Lord' (Leviticus, I, II), I lost interest; and whenever the teacher was due, I would disappear into the courtyard, returning only after being called many times in vain by my mother. In this manner, half the time of the scheduled lesson was lost, while my teacher waited for me with the Bible open at exactly the same page where he had left off translating the sacrifices – of which there seemed to be no end.

What I found most curious about my teacher was that although he was very tall, his name was Kurz, meaning 'short' in English. (From the end of the eighteenth century, Jews throughout the Austro-Hungarian Empire, which also included a large part of Poland, were forced to take German names for census purposes. Corrupt officials graded the names according to the amount of bribe offered. A scale was established starting at the top with names such as 'Diamant', 'Brilliant', decreasing with 'Gold', 'Silber', 'Holz', and ending with the German equivalents for Blue, Green, Black, White to which 'stein' (stone), 'feld' (field), and 'mann' (man) were often added. Names of towns such as Krakauer and Warschauer or trades such as Schneider (tailor) and Schuster (shoemaker) were also sold. People who would or could not pay were given derogatory names such as Klein (small) or Unkraut (weed). Huge amounts were paid by the Cohens and Levis who were thus able to circumvent the regulation and preserve their Jewish names. The fact that Jews in Europe could be identified immediately upon presentation of documents bearing the 'purchased' names was of great value to the Germans in the execution of the mass murder organized by them during the Second World War).[10]

When Mr Kurz failed, my father took my religious education into his own hands. He taught me how to pray. On pain of being slapped, I was to recite by heart Hebrew prayers I had learned to read in German characters. I had to wear a 'yarmulke' (skull cap), but only during meals and prayers. The gentiles were not to see the cap because it might incite them to beat me up. The whole thing was incomprehensible to me, but under the threat of punishment, I learned to do things I neither understood nor liked.

Mr Kurz's face showed astonishment when I met him in Haifa twenty years later. As if he were surprised that I was still alive. He did not share my joy in meeting someone from back home, probably because he still resented my behaviour as a child or perhaps because having become the owner of a metal shop, he suspected that the survivor of the 'holocaust' was after some sort of assistance.

When I began to go to grammar school, I was exempted from writing on Saturday. So, not having been beaten up because of the yarmulke, I was chased and beaten by my gentile comrades for having been granted the privilege of not having to do any writing on Saturdays. I wished to be like them, free of yarmulkes and special regulations. I wanted to be one of them.

We used the word 'comrade', because that was what fellow pupils were called in Germany and Austria. We were supposed to be comrades. Starting from the lowest grades, we were enrolled in the youth movement of the Vaterlaendische Front (Front of the Father Land) organized along lines similar to the Hitlerjugend (Hitler Youth Movement) in Germany. I was allowed to wear the badge with the slogan 'Be United', but not the uniform.

By then, I realized that uniforms provided protection. Like the yarmulke. If you wore it, God would protect you. If you didn't, a stone might fall from Heaven and kill you. If you said your prayers every day, God would reward you. But if you entered the church together with your friends, the roof might come down and kill you. Till this day, I have never entered a church again. I still wear the yarmulke occasionally; but having lost its protective power, I still crave a uniform. Badges, uniforms, insignia, signs of rank, stars of gold and silver, worn by military personnel and policemen, all were coveted; while lions, bears and eagles inspired me with awe whenever they appeared on flags or coats of arms, or were embedded in the masonry of ancient city gates and castles.

Like the other boys, I secretly started making paper swastikas which were being scattered in buses, trams and other public places. It was our maid, the policeman's sister, who caught me at it. She promised not to tell my father, if I promised not to do it again. In those days of winter 1937, the National Socialist party was still illegal in Austria and whoever was caught distributing pictures of Hitler or little flags with swastikas was severely punished. The sign – the pictures on the covers of illustrated papers showing it in its fascinating majesty being carried on multitudes of flags through the streets of Germany by thousands of soldiers – was a constant source of envy to me, the little 'Saujud' (Jew-pig) who was not even allowed to cut it out of paper.

Of course, we had the *Magen David* (Star of David), but that was neither carried through the streets on flags nor were you allowed to wear it on your lapel. My mother wore one, but she always hid it carefully under her dress. My little brother was allowed to touch it. He was still sitting on her lap at times, and she used to tell him stories about her father who had been a very pious rabbi to whom people from all over Poland would come to seek advice. How she had cried when he died and when her mother died soon afterwards of a broken heart.

I had no use for such stories. I wanted martial music, flags, parades and drums.

HITLER

My father's practice was very lucrative. During the years in which my mother was purchase manager, people used to complain to her about their pains and illnesses, and she would steer them to her husband for treatment. As his income grew, she left her job and started handling his accounts. She used to tell with pride how he received an average of forty patients a day, not counting the many house calls he would make in the evenings, riding his bicycle through Innsbruck where cars were rare.

My father loved to tell about an accident he had had on one of his rounds when the Christian god knocked his teeth out. He had accidentally ridden right into the statue's wooden toes sticking out from the huge crucifix which dominated the little square off the road. The implication was that the Christian god had taken his revenge for having been nailed to the cross, a sin which was carried by every Jew and a guilt accepted and handed down from father to son wherever assimilation had taken root in exchange for emancipation.

My first contact with Christianity was in grammer school at the age of six when I had to stand up every morning while the others recited the 'Vater Unser' ('The Lord's Prayer'). Jesus Christus was the father they were praying to, and we – the Jews – had killed him. His figure, with blood running from his hands and feet, was nailed to a cross and hung above the blackboard.

It was not until the Sixties, when I was selling tyres in West Africa, that I was able to turn the accusation against the accuser. As I sat alone with our agent in

Onitsha after everyone else had left a party celebrating a successful business deal, he invited me to stay for the night; and over a bottle of beer, he put his arm around my shoulder and asked, 'Now tell me David, seeing that we are such good friends, why did you kill Jesus?'

I had no trouble answering him, 'Now imagine that a man came to the Onitsha market, got on a crate and started speaking to the crowd saying that it is easier for a camel to go through a needle's eye than for a rich man to go to the kingdom of Heaven. What would you do?'

'I'd kill 'im!'

When I started laughing, he realized that I had quoted Jesus and that he, the Christian, had assumed the role of judge and executioner to punish someone who had made a verbal attack on the rich, of whom he was one.

However, in late 1937, neither Jesus nor the constant talk of war had any effect on my father, the doctor, who counted many prominent citizens and even some members of the secret National Socialist party among his patients. He used to tell us at the dinner table that even they thought that Hitler would not dare come to Austria. And if he did, he might do something against the 'Ostjuden' (Jews from eastern Europe) because of their ugly garb and their repulsive manners; but to a respectable physician treating forty people a day, nothing would happen.

He bought a plot of land right next to the church; but when the church authorities informed him that they would oppose the erection of a house owned by a Jew adjacent to the church, he sold it and bought another one a few blocks away. At first, it was to be a villa; but since foundation and roof wouldn't cost much more than for a villa, a

14

three-storey apartment house was planned – construction to begin March 15, 1938.

My mother wouldn't hear of it. She was afraid. Another war was going to come, so who needed houses. 'Let's go to Palestine,' she used to repeat over and over again, but my father wouldn't listen to her. When she cried, he told her to stop snivelling in front of us. The leaders of the world were reading the papers too. There would be no other war. And anyway, Hitler was just bragging.

He nearly had me convinced – a boy of nearly ten – but then coming home from school one day, I entered the dining room and found my father, my mother with my brother on her lap, and Amalia sitting around the radio staring at the little yellow light and listening intently. I was just about to close the door when my father's 'sshh!' made me stop. 'Hitler is speaking!' he intoned gravely, and it sounded as if he had said that God was speaking. The family facing the radio was like the gentiles when praying before meals to the family crucifix which hung in every dining room together with garlands of wheat or cobs of corn.

Hitler speaks!

His raucous voice rose above the crackling of the radio. The yellow light flickered at times, and then came the shout arising from thousands of throats like a huge waterfall – 'Heil! Heil!' Ebbing and rising again. The radio was shut off. Lunch was served. And my mother cried.

A few days later, the Germans came. The plot was sold back to the contractor at a loss. Amalia had to go. A Jew was not allowed to employ a German – that was clear even before the new laws came into force. Jewish doctors were not allowed to treat German patients, but my father held that this would probably not be applied in Austria. After all, who would treat all my father's patients, if he were not allowed to practise any more? That's what it would have amounted to, seeing that only about one hundred Jewish families lived in Innsbruck. Some of them were already planning to emigrate. The word '*Jude*' was smeared all over my father's name-plates and our door, not to be removed by order of the police.

Lunch and dinner turned into rows. My mother would plead for us to leave everything and go, but she was told not to be hysterical like her mother.

'Where to?' he would shout, 'where to?!'

'Anywhere.' Tears would run down her cheeks, with my little brother joining in, bringing tears to my eyes too, because I was afraid that he would hit her again.

'Don't snivel!' he roared. He raised his arm and brought it down, smashing the plate with the handle of the knife in his fist.

My mother scurried to pick up the pieces, repeating, 'Anywhere, just anywhere.'

'You are stupid! One needs a visa!'

'It isn't true. People just leave and go over the border. They leave everything and go.'

From conversations that my mother had with neighbours, I learned that visas could be had for a lot of money but only to countries where our father would not be allowed to practise medicine. The Christian neighbours assured my mother that her husband was right and that there was no need to run away. Even Mrs Hardt, who was from the Reich, had said that Jews like Dr Haber would not have to leave. Maybe the others. Her husband was with the Gestapo, so she had to know. I wasn't told what 'Gestapo' meant, but the word was always whispered with awe and fear.

My mother did not smile any more. Hans was no longer allowed to sit on her lap. The curtains were drawn so that I would not watch the Jungvolk (youngsters of eight to fourteen years old – organized within the Hitler Youth Movement) marching past with drums and trumpets celebrating their victories.

The heavy atmosphere at home did not prevent me from getting caught up in the continual festive mood of the town. At school, my friends were proudly wearing their Hitlerjugend uniforms, talking about parades and military training they were receiving and about no longer having to attend catechism lessons. Only those whose parents insisted had to attend.

Not being allowed to wear a uniform myself, I took to hanging around the square near the central railway station. I memorized all the different uniforms worn by officers and other German dignitaries arriving from Germany in an endless stream. At times, a detachment of SS (Schutzstaffeln, body guard echelons) or SA (Sturmabteilungen, storm troopers) would march past in black or brown, or the Hitlerjugend, whom I admired most, would pass with their drums and fifes behind the flag bearers.

Secretly, I started drawing flags and skulls with bones only to tear them up lest I be found out and beaten by my father. But there was to be no flag for me to follow.

It was too late to get baptized, as so many Jews had done before. However, my father said repeatedly that the new laws were for the baptized too, so they hadn't gained anything after all. If he had chosen to be baptized at the time, the church would have allowed him to build his house next door to them; but it was too late, and the house would have been Aryanized anyway. Had his great grandparents been baptized, he might have been an Aryan; but, as my mother so wisely remarked, had her grandmother been on wheels, she would have been a bus.

RESCUE

One morning, Mrs Goldenberg, who was our next-door neighbour, committed suicide. While they were having breakfast, she told her husband and her boy Freddy that she was only going down to fetch some bread; but instead of going downstairs, she climbed up to the last floor and jumped into the street. They called an ambulance, but it was too late. She was dead.

As my mother told the story over lunch, I must have turned white, because she asked me if I felt all right.

'Of course I feel all right,' I said immediately, fearing that if I said that I didn't, I would have had to follow my father to the surgery to be examined. But my heart was beating quickly and I was very much afraid. I was trembling without understanding why. I felt as if my mother was suddenly dead, and I was afraid that she too might tell us that she was only going down to fetch some bread and then jump from the fourth floor. But she continued serving the meal, while my father read the paper.

When she told him again that we had to go, he got up and left the room, slamming the door behind him.

'Soon it will be over,' my mother said, and again I started

trembling because I thought she meant to do the same as Mrs Goldenberg. However, what she meant was something else. A few days later, we were told: Mr Gudin, a very rich contractor from Lithuania who used to come every year to Austria to get treated by my father for varicose veins, had finally been able to obtain a visa through the intervention of Lithuania's Prime Minister, Merkys. He, too, had been treated once by my father, who had made a special trip to Zurich where the Prime Minister was taking a cure.

The visa was only for my father, who was to go to Lithuania at once, while my mother, brother and I were to follow later. First, he had to find a flat for us and for his practice; and only after my mother would sell whatever could be sold, were we to follow him to Kovno.

We were told that Mr Gudin had saved us; and out of gratitude, my father would teach his son, who was studying medicine, the secret of the drug he had developed for eliminating varicose veins – my father's special field.

However, the elder Mr Gudin was deported by the Russians to Siberia in 1940, and his son became captain of police in the Kovno Ghetto in 1941. Twenty-five years later, on a business trip to Australia, I was asked by someone if I had heard about Gudin, the police captain of the Kovno Ghetto, who now lived in Melbourne. I said I had never heard of him. It was the least I could do for the man whose father had saved us, but it was more than that. There was to be no confrontation. Nobody in the Melbourne of 1965 needed to know about my father's role in the Kovno Ghetto, which the younger Mr Gudin remembered as well as I did.

KRISTALLNACHT

While my mother went about selling our belongings and father's various bits of apparatus, we were placed with a Jewish family who lived near the railway station. I slept in the pantry and my brother was on the sofa in the dining room. Mr Landauer prayed every morning, donning his tallis (prayer shawl) and tefillin (phylacteries), and said the blessing after every meal. He kept repeating that no harm would come to anyone who prayed.

After having sold most of the medical instruments and equipment and having packed and crated furniture and carpets, my mother went to Vienna to collect the visa. When my father had gone to Lithuania, I felt nothing. He had just gone on a trip. However, when my mother went to Vienna where she was to wait for a week or more for the documents to be processed, I became frightened. I still remembered the stories they told about the Jews in Vienna who had to scrub the sidewalks with soap and water while the SA men beat them. What if they caught my mother? I was worried that she might do the same thing Mrs Goldenberg had done.

I could not sleep, and being alone in the pantry made me even more afraid. I tried to sleep, but I wasn't tired enough because I was no longer allowed to go to school or go outside while mother was away. Every creak, every sound of steps on the staircase made me reach for my pen-knife which I kept open under the pillow.

I must have fallen asleep after all, when suddenly I felt myself surrounded in darkness with shouting, screaming, and sounds of breaking glass. At first, I did not know whether I was dreaming, but the noise did not stop. Slowly, I began to realize that there were strangers in the house – maybe burglars – and then I heard Mrs Landauer scream. I did not dare to put the light on. Hiding under the covers, I clutched my penknife in my fist, ready to stick it into anybody who came into the room. But nobody came in. Gradually the noises ceased. There was one last slam of the front door and the sound of steps running down the stairs.

I tried to go to sleep again, but I stared into the darkness until it became grey outside. Only then did I dress and go into the dining room. Everything was broken. Plates, chairs, upholstered furniture ripped open.

As I am describing this, almost sixty years after the 9th of November 1938, I wonder why it was the destruction of the room which struck me first and not the people in it. During the night of November 9 until the next day, SA and SS units raided Jewish homes throughout Germany. 'Property was destroyed, 20,000 Jews had been taken into 'protective custody', half of them being sent to Buchenwald camp. There had been 36 Jews killed and 36 badly wounded.'[11]

Only when Mrs Landauer started screaming again and my brother crying, did I realize that there was somebody else in the room besides myself.

'Here, see his tallis. It is all covered with blood!'

Mrs Landauer held out the tallis for me to see, but I just stood there. All I thought was – where was der liebe Gott ('the kind God' as He used to be called in German) who was supposed to help the ones who prayed?

The yarmulke, the tallis and the tefillin had not kept the Germans from taking Mr Landauer into 'protective custody'. He had wanted to take his tallis with him, but they didn't let him.

'You don't need it where you are going,' they said and beat him until his face was full of blood.

I kept staring at the dark brown stains. I was afraid to look Mrs Landauer in the face, because she continued crying while my brother stood next to her holding her hand as if she were his mother.

'Stop snivelling!' I thought.

It was at that moment that I felt abandoned for the first time in my life. My mother had gone to Vienna. My father was already forgotten. Mr Landauer, whom I had watched swaying back and forth in prayer, was probably dead. And yet, I did not cry. On the contrary, I became very angry. Not with anybody in particular, but just terribly angry.

The world became a stage with me the only spectator. The feeling that nobody really existed, that all the others were strangers who could harm me, pervaded me completely, persisting with few exceptions throughout the years.

The only thing I feared was physical pain; while death, not yet having manifested itself in my presence, remained an idea to be dreaded. Everything would disappear, with me being buried under a lot of earth weighing heavily on my chest – unable to breathe, unable to see anything anymore.

LITHUANIA

KOVNO

We arrived in Lithuania in November 1938.

My father's practice grew. Patients were received in the dining room while we were at school, but most of his work was done during house-calls which the richer Jews of Kovno preferred. Mr Gudin had not only found the flat for us in one of the buildings he owned, but his recommendations brought many patients – both Jewish and gentile – to our home.

There was no problem with the Jewish patients, because they all spoke Yiddish which both my parents knew well, having spoken the language as children. However, the non-Jews spoke Lithuanian, a language none of us had ever heard. Nevertheless, this problem was also overcome. My mother had been raised in Poland and still remembered Polish, so the new maid we had just hired was able to translate from Polish to Lithuanian. The patients talked to her, and she in turn translated for my mother, who conveyed the people's complaints to my father.

My mother collected the fees, saving most of the income to buy a new flat. Mr Gudin had advised us to move to a more fashionable neighbourhood in order to get higher-class patients.

My brother and I went back to school.

Out of a population of 140,000 in Kovno, 40,000 were Jews. There were numerous Jewish grammar schools, five high schools, three of which were conducted in Hebrew with a pronounced Zionist background. One taught in Yiddish; another in Lithuanian to provide education for those Jews who considered themselves 'Lithuanians of the Jewish faith'. The old city abounded with synagogues and Jewish institutions flourished. The cultural needs of the Jewish population were fulfilled with Yiddish and Hebrew newspapers, theatres and social services. In Slobodka, a suburb of Kovno, one of the most famous 'yeshivas' of Eastern Europe attracted students from all over the world. On our way to the Hebrew high school, my brother and I were surprised to see the many signs with Hebrew letters on shops and billboards.

What impressed me most about school was that no prayers were recited in the morning, there were no uniforms, and there were lots of girls. Boys and girls studying in the same school was something new to me.

Our arrival was an event. We were called the refugees from Germany, and our association with danger evoked endless curiosity. Almost daily, I was encouraged by my fellow students to stand on top of the teacher's desk during class break to tell the story of how the Germans had smashed the furniture and beaten Mr Landauer until he bled and how they had dragged him down the stairs. To increase my popularity, I started to embellish the story by inventing details that had never happened. I called upon my brother to testify to their truth, since he had seen it all from under the sofa where he had hidden the moment the Nazis started banging on the door.

Stories of atrocities and sufferings inflicted upon Jews

living somewhere else were as popular then as they are today. Listeners and readers felt fortunate not to be there.

I am always reminded of those school appearances every time I observe my fellow Jews in Israel craving for news – any news, on the hour – on buses, at home, in the office, and as a crowning treat, on the nine o'clock television newscast. If no Jew is murdered that day, then there is nothing on the news of any interest. To fill news vacuums created by the lack of Jewish suffering and to satisfy the need to feel guilty about being Jewish, the media pours accusation upon accusation of invented or exaggerated Jewish atrocities against Arabs and brings them into Jewish homes on a never-ending conveyor belt in order to create the ancient and emotionally comfortable feeling of guilt which has contaminated Jewish souls throughout the centuries.

The lack of understanding with which my stories were received when I was eleven years old almost matches that of today's television viewers, who seem unable to distinguish between those daily shows being passed off as reality and reality being represented as a continuous show – easy to watch as a spectator without involvement – with the ability to change Jews burnt alive in a bus into a musical at the touch of the remote control button.

In the winter of 1938–39, one only had to change the subject. The war in Finland was something people saw in the newsreels during their weekly visits to the cinema. Something as far removed as the war between the Japanese and the Chinese, with their towns burning and people fleeing, could be seen in photographs displayed with the latest movie posters such as Metro-Goldwyn-Mayer's *Anna Karenina* – a bizarre juxtaposition of harsh reality and fantasy.

Although Finland was almost 'next door' and money was being collected to support the war against the communists, the Jews of Kovno still believed in the 'peace in our time' promised by Prime Minister Chamberlain of Great Britain, the country with the most powerful fleet in the world. Before Hitler came to power, Jews considered anything German to be superior. Now the Jews looked up to England which had promised to 'give' them Palestine. Chaim Weizmann, prominent scientist and president of the World Zionist Organization for many years, lived in England and would see to it that the promise was kept.

Another feature characterizing Jewish activities was the abundance of youth movements. Every faction of Zionism sponsored a youth movement, which in one way or another was inspired by the idea of Palestine, or 'Eretz Yisrael' (Land of Israel) as it was generally called. In spite of the fact that not many people above thirty seriously considered going to Palestine, all the younger people looked upon it not just as a place of refuge from persecution, but a place to start a new life. Jewish youths did not differ in that way from all the other young people who adopted the ideas of right-wing fascism or left-wing communism in their various forms.

It was, therefore, natural for me to soon find my way to the movement most suitable to satisfy my craving for marching in formation and a uniform. The fact that 'Betar' (abbreviation for 'Brith Joseph Trumpeldor') advocated the conquest of Palestine by military means added ideological attraction to the youth branch of Zeev Jabotinsky's Zionist-Revisionist movement. Its aim was to 'create the "normal" citizen, or, the "healthy" one, of the Jewish nation – in the State of the Jews.'[12]

As my mother handled all money matters, I asked her

for the amount needed to cover my membership fee; and she gave it to me without asking any questions. She knew that every Friday afternoon I went to the Betar. My father, who was present only at meals, took no interest in my extra-curricular activities, seeing that my grades were acceptable and that I had quickly grasped the Hebrew and Lithuanian languages with the aid of a private teacher.

The competing fund-raising drives of the various Zionist factions were reaching their peak. The imminent danger of war, which became more acute after the German annexation of Czechoslovakia at the end of 1938, aroused the fears of the Jewish population who, dreading their future, quite suddenly began taking a greater interest in Palestine.

A great controversy developed. Should the funds be used to acquire more land in Palestine, acre by acre, or should they be used for the financing of illegal immigration to circumvent – or fight if necessary – the naval blockade instituted by the British government to enforce the restrictions placed upon Jewish immigration in accordance with the White Paper of 1939 allowing only 75,000 Jews within the next five years into Palestine?

At school, the controversy took the form of fist fights resulting from the students grabbing and breaking the collection boxes, while the adults gave their support to various political groups whose conflicting aims and views were disseminated through vituperative articles published in Jewish newspapers. The heated arguments and the violent enmities that ensued often created rifts or even break-ups of family and friendships.

When Jabotinsky arrived in Kovno shortly before the outbreak of the Second World War, everyone understood his warning that 'if we don't liquidate the exile, the exile will liquidate us', but it was not heeded. His call for the evacuation of the European Jews was attacked by almost every Zionist leader. The whole machinery of the World Zionist Organization was mobilized to counter his 'alarmist, hysterical, fascistic and militaristic' views; particularly after Dr Chaim Weizmann had officially declared while on a visit to Poland that:

> Palestine was no solution for the Jewish problem of Europe . . . we want only the best of Jewish youth to come to us. We want only people of education to enter Palestine for the purpose of increasing its culture. The other Jews will have to stay where they are and face whatever fate awaits them. These millions of Jews are dust on the wheels of history and have to be blown away. We don't want them pouring into Palestine. We don't want our Tel Aviv to become another low-grade ghetto.[13]

I had not been allowed to take part in the Betar parade in which 800 uniformed members were inspected by Jabotinsky himself on his arrival at the Kovno airport. My mother had secretly given me money to buy a uniform shirt, but we could not risk father finding out. My private teacher, himself an active revisionist, was also strangely opposed to my taking part in the parade. If my father should find out, it could mean that I would lose my 'freedom' on Friday afternoons.

Unfortunately, a few days later, I forgot to hide the Betar badge with the symbol of the 'menorah' which I always wore at school. When my father discovered that I had become a member of the Betar, he beat me severely, after chasing me around the dinner table, and called me 'dirty dog, Nazi!'.

It was quite common in those days for Jews to call their political opponents Nazis, just as it is today in Israel when 'the Likud accuses Labor of using Stuermer-style Nazi propaganda in its Histadrut [Workers' Union] election campaign'.[14] However, the epithets coming from my own father went far beyond the beating I had expected. To him I really was a 'Nazi'. The blue trimmings on our brown uniform were not enough to withstand his comparison with Hitler's brown shirted SA. A German marching tune, composed before the Nazis came to power, was sung by us enthusiastically with Hebrew words. I taught it to my brother and we sang it at night, silently, in order not to wake our parents. But then, one day, the song was broadcast on the German radio, sung by German soldiers, marching off to Poland.

'Did you hear that?'

'What?'

'That song the Germans sang. That song your filthy Nazi son was singing the other night!'

My mother kept silent.

I was forbidden to leave the house on Friday afternoons. My uniform, which I had kept at the club, was given to a boy whose parents were too poor to afford one. So I went back to drawing not only uniforms but planes, exploding bombs and burning houses.

The war had started.

FIRE

To prevent me from returning to the Betar, the private teacher was instructed to supervise my Friday afternoon activities. This he did by taking me on extensive walks through the town, during which he explained the strategic implications of the invasion of Poland by both Germany and Russia and how Jabotinsky was right in preaching evacuation. He said that any day the Russians or the Germans might decide to grab the Baltic states and that therefore, anyone in his right mind had to run away. The Russians would try to get back what they considered to be theirs (the Baltic States were part of Russia before the communists took power there in 1917) and the Germans would finally set out to conquer their coveted 'Lebensraum' in the East and try to get to Leningrad through Lithuania, Latvia and Estonia. Looking at the map, it all made good sense, but most important were the words of Jabotinsky, repeated over and over again in public speeches, pamphlets and newspaper articles: 'Jews! If you won't liquidate the exile, the exile will liquidate *you*!' Those words were turning from a prophetic warning into reality. From all over eastern Europe came reports of increasing anti-semitic excesses. Encouraged by the German atrocities in Poland, the populace, often with the connivance of the authorities, openly terrorized the Jewish population in Hungary, Rumania and Slovakia. Even we had to move about in pairs to protect ourselves against attacks by Lithuanians. When Jabotinsky started warning, right after the First World War, against what the exile held in store – the conflagration of anti-semitism all over Europe, where attacks on Jews, especially in eastern Europe, were constantly taking place, the Jews dismissed them as 'isolated incidents'. Now, the Jews of Kovno dismissed them as unthinkable in Lithuania. Yet, to move about alone was dangerous.

My teacher disappeared one day before the summer

vacation of 1940. My mother told me that he had phoned her before he left for Palestine to wish me all the best.

Similar to the way I was asked to tell my stories as a 'German refugee' to my class in school, Jewish refugees from Poland were now being interviewed by the Jewish press, which brought daily accounts of the horrors of Jewish suffering. Money was raised, blankets were collected, every social service was engaged in relieving the plight which had befallen those fortunate to have escaped, yet unfortunate to have become destitute and dependent on charity. With their whole hearts, the Jews of Kovno donated and helped in every way, hoping in this manner to avert a similar fate which had already started to loom on the horizon.

Not many took the few remaining ways out. One could still escape by secretly crossing into Russian-occupied Poland and from there to Rumania where Jewish organizations helped escapees to go to Palestine. Communists could go to Russia. False visas to central American countries were traded almost openly and enabled people to get to Sweden – 'in transit'.

When my mother raised the subject, she was told what almost everybody thought: that those things were only good for youngsters. But the youngsters too, except for a few who, like my teacher, took the road to Bucharest, parroted their elders' admonitions about the dangers and their professed faith in the German-Russian non-aggression pact. Blind to what went on around them, deaf to warnings by those who knew better, they went about their daily occupations, hoping.

My mother continued pleading: 'Let's leave! Let's leave everything behind and leave! Anywhere! Anyhow!'

This time the arguments were more subdued. No plates were smashed. No fists were raised – instead, father gave political lectures. He said that Hitler had made a pact with Russia. He would not expose himself to a war on two fronts. He just could not afford it. And the Russians did not need Lithuania. Having taken Vilna from the the Poles, they were even talking about giving it back to Lithuania. We are a bit like Switzerland – so the Prime Minister himself had told him. And anyway, Palestine was only for the poor and those without education or a profession.

There was nothing to fear. Just as we had done the year before, we went with everyone else to spend the summer at Palanga, the most fashionable sea resort in Lithuania. I did not enjoy the sea, nor did I share my brother's delight in watching jellyfish disintegrate once out of the water or his joy in finding real amber.

I wanted to be with Zelda, the girl I used to walk home with after school, with my brother following at a distance so that we could talk without being disturbed. She knew all about the fights at home and my mother's fears which I had come to share.

Although her eyes were green and not brown like my mother's, she always reminded me of her – maybe because of her name. However, I somehow was never able to say it, so I called her by her family name of Kuzne as everyone else did at school. When I walked home with her, she was just 'you'. Only in bed at night when everything was over, I called her Zelda. I called out to her because something terrible had happened; something I could not talk about to anybody, something I could tell only to her.

A few days before the summer vacation, my brother and I were on our way home, when all of a sudden I noticed dense black smoke rising from a few streets further ahead. As we approached the intersection, I saw to my right a smoke stack emitting a thin puff of vapour. I thought that the smoke had stopped, but then my brother cried out! As I turned to my left, I saw the fire. A huge building was burning from the bottom up. Flames reaching out from the windows joined those engulfing the roof and disappeared in rolling clouds of smoke hiding the sky.

I started to tremble. All of a sudden I remembered the Temple in Jerusalem and the things my mother had told me when she fasted on Tisha B'Av (the ninth of Av, the date in the Hebrew calendar on which both Temples were destroyed in Jerusalem). The Romans had burned the Temple, and the Jews had perished in the fire. Nobody could get out; nobody could escape; all were trapped within the walls of Jerusalem, and those who were not burned – including the small children – were killed by the Romans with their swords. That was what my mother had told me, and that was what I saw before my eyes as I lay in bed in Palanga fearing that one day the flames would consume Zelda and me. I feared that I would not get to see her again, that I would die like the Jews in Jerusalem, that they would kill us all in the Temple (synagogue) while we were praying. I swore in my heart never again to go to the Temple although my father still forced me to do so occasionally.

Stories were going around about how the Germans had killed whole villages in Poland, but those were probably exaggerations by the refugees who wanted more money. I didn't think so though. If the Romans had done it in Jerusalem, there was no reason why the Germans would not do it in Poland. That is why they went there in the first place – to kill as many as possible and take their money and their homes. They might come to Lithuania, too.

The thoughts never ceased. The nights never ended. At times, I was still able to conjure Zelda's face in the darkness; but as time went by, I could not do so as often as I wished. There always came the flames reminding me that one day I would have to die. One day, sooner or later, one day, no matter what I would be doing or where I would be going, I would not be able to see or feel anything any more – except the earth weighing heavily on my chest, on my face, preventing me from getting up again. Why was I alive, I asked myself, if I had to die anyway? It made no sense. I was twelve years old.

STALIN

Overnight, everything changed. Music. Red flags everywhere. And tanks. Tanks with red stars painted on their sides like those we had seen on the newsreel photographs in the cinema showcases. Column after column blocked our train in which we were hurrying home to our luxurious flat in Kovno. My parents feared that it might be occupied by the Russians, who had finally entered Lithuania.

'A master stroke,' my father declared. 'Stalin – one of the greatest leaders of our times.'

'But they are communists!' my mother exclaimed.

'Shut up! So what?! We are German citizens. They won't touch us!'

He brandished his passport bearing the German eagle

spreading its wings above a wreath surrounding the swastika with a big red 'J' for Jude (Jew) stamped below it.

A decree was published on October 5, 1938, only a week after the Munich agreement, which required the passports of Jews to be stamped with the letter 'J' . . . The advice, which was to enable the German authorities in occupied Europe to identify and capture many thousands of Jewish refugees, was the creation of a foreign and neutralist government. Heinrich Rothmund, the Swiss federal Chief of Police, was to check the flood of Jewish immigrants into Switzerland, and to do so without harming the tourist traffic from Germany by the re-introduction of the visa system. Rothmund went to Berlin in person and there, on September 27, 1938, he signed the 'J-stamp' agreement, together with Werner Best, the Gestapo's legal expert, and Gustav Roediger of the Foreign Office's consulate section.[15]

I was memorizing the shapes of the tanks to draw them later. I did not like the drab uniforms of the Russian soldiers, nor those of their officers without shoulder tabs. But easier to draw, I thought, as I memorized the insignia and the red star with the crossed hammer and sickle.

As the cab took us home from the station. I wondered where all the red flags had come from. They were flying from every building. Every house flew at least one, and Stalin's face smiled at us from every shop window. Loudspeakers had been installed on every street corner. Martial music and Russian folk dances blared alternately, only occasionally interrupted by the shout 'Hurrah!' after some unintelligible speech. It reminded me of the 'Heil' following all the speeches on the German radio, to which my father still faithfully listened every morning after laying tefillin.

Huge billboards appeared on every street with pictures of Marx, Engels, Lenin and Stalin arranged like postage stamps against the background of red banners reading 'Proletarians of the World Unite!'.

Was my father a proletarian? His patient, former Prime Minister Antanas Merkys, had been deported to Siberia, and the President of the former Republic of Lithuania, Antanas Smetona, had fled to Germany. Mr Gudin was afraid that he would be deported any day. All his holdings had been nationalized, leaving him in the post of manager of a small brick factory which he had formerly owned.

My father stopped seeing him, lest he be suspected of bourgeois leanings. After all, he was a member of a free profession and not an 'exploiter of the working class' as was Mr Gudin. Upon the recommendation of two of his patients who had been secret members of the Communist Party, outlawed before the arrival of the Russians, my father had immediately applied and been accepted for membership in the Communist Professional Union of Physicians. A map of Asia, showing in red all the sixteen Soviet Socialist Republics of Russia, now took up the wall where the portraits of my grandparents had once hung. German versions of the complete works of Marx, Engels, Lenin and Stalin and the history of the Communist Party of the USSR occupied the bookshelves below the map where medical works had once been kept.

I was sent to a different school. The Jewish school system was dismantled. All private schools were nationalized, and students were enrolled in education centres nearest to their homes. Tuition was free and so was medical care. My father was now paid by the Government for each patient treated, according to invoices made out by my mother.

I became active in the public affairs of the new school. My drawing talents were soon recognized, and I was invited to join the editorial board of the class newspaper. I drew Lenin addressing the workers during the revolution and the storming of the Winter Palace – all copied from newspapers and history books, neatly coloured and dramatically enhanced with flames and the ever-flying red flags in the background or right in front of the victorious Red Army. The army to whom we had to be grateful, as my father said, for our 'deliverance'.

It was prohibited to speak Hebrew. Only Yiddish, Lithuanian or Russian were allowed. So we spoke Yiddish. In spite of the fact that Yiddish had become the language of instruction at school, my father did not suffer me to speak it over the phone when patients were there. He said that it would spoil my German, but I knew that he just did not want the high-ranking Russian officers – who now filled the waiting room and used the bathtub as a urinal, leaving the door wide open to the consternation of my mother – to think that he was anything but a doctor who had fled from Germany because he was a communist. It was unfashionable and even dangerous to be a Jew, particularly a religious one partaking in 'the opium of the people' as Marx described religion.

My father decided that we did not need a superior 'Policeman' to watch over us from above and, therefore, exempted me from prayers and the yarmulke. One evening at the dinner table when my mother had repeated once more that we had to run away before it was too late and was told that she was a stupid cow, he took the yarmulke off my head.

37

I felt naked without it. I remembered the admonishment that a stone might fall from Heaven, but it was more than that. There was nothing any more to hold on to. I never did admit to my friends from the Betar or even to Zelda that I believed that God would help me. Even when trying to conjure up her face at night, I prayed to God that He should keep the flames away from me, that our house should not catch fire or be bombed as in Warsaw or be burned like the Temple in Jerusalem. I never asked myself whether He spoke German.

God having been discharged of His duties as 'Superior Policeman', I was left only with Zelda's increasingly blurred image before my eyes. She had disappeared and nobody knew to which school she had been sent. One day, I saw her in the street. She had grown taller than I, and she was wearing a bra. My heart started beating very fast, and I was too scared to even say hello. She just passed me by.

A few weeks later, I saw her again with one of my former friends. I flew into a rage. Wielding my knife, I rushed to stab him, but somebody grabbed me from behind and wrested the knife from my hand.

'One day,' I raged in silence, 'I'll get you! Both of you!'

I faintly remembered the commandment 'Thou shalt not kill', but it had become irrelevant. The 'Superior Policeman' was no longer watching.

Our dining room was divided from the surgery by a heavy wooden sliding door, which was locked at all times. I was told to do my homework there in order not to be disturbed by my brother in the children's room.

I would try to study, but I was often interrupted by the sound of moaning from the other side of the door whenever someone was given an injection or some other painful treatment. The sounds of medical instruments clattering on glass or my mother being called to translate Russian into German via Polish always broke my train of thought.

My curiosity was aroused one day when I thought I recognized the voice of a woman having a subdued conversation with my father. I looked through the keyhole and saw him kneeling in front of her, while she sat on the couch holding his head between her hands. They got up, put their arms around each other, kissed, and after she had smoothed her dress which had gone up above her knees, he called my mother.

What supposedly had been a medical consultation now became a social visit. The lady's name was Mrs Serebrovicz. Her husband, Joseph Kaspi-Serebrovicz, was in prison. Before the annexation, he had been the advertising manager of the *Yiddishe Shtime*, a widely circulated Jewish daily. The job had been very lucrative considering that the placement of commercial advertisements in advantageous spots brought under-the-table payments which far exceeded a manager's salary.

Being a Revisionist-Zionist, Mr Serebrovicz occasionally published articles mostly aimed at the Kovno Jewish leftists whom he had branded Stalin's stooges when the *Shtime*'s workers had asked for higher wages. He was denounced and imprisoned within a week of Kovno's occupation by the Red Army.

His wife and two daughters were left penniless. Having been among the richer patients before her husband's arrest, she now became my father's ward. Her swollen veins had been healed, and she now only came for consultation. Otherwise, her visits would have aroused suspicion about the doctor's association with the enemies of the working class – a thing one could not afford. My father told my mother that the money he hid in German books which Mrs Serebrovicz borrowed was given out of 'rachmones' (pity, compassion). I gathered from eavesdropping that the books were part of the German education Mrs Serebrovicz was receiving from my father, who was teaching her how to pronounce the umlauts. My mother did not suspect any infringement of the tenth commandment and warmly received Mrs Serebrovicz, who occasionally brought her daughters with her. My mother even praised her beauty.

Although I wore the red scarf of the pioneers, I never forgot that I was a Betari who had sworn to go to Palestine and fight for a Jewish State. I pressed my lips together tightly when the oath solemnly declaring 'in the presence of my comrades to fight for the cause of Lenin and Stalin' was taken at a public function at school. When I was questioned about my silence, I gave the excuse that it was because of a toothache.

Eli Segal, my best friend who had introduced me to the Betar, and I had sworn to each other that in spite of the interdict against speaking Hebrew, we would continue to do so and that we would go to Palestine – come what may. We still spoke Hebrew to each other when we met four years later at the 'Entlausung' (delousing) at 'Arbeitslager Eins', which belonged to the Dachau concentration camp complex. I still do. Only Eli is no longer here. He fell in 1948 commanding a unit of the Irgun Zvai Leumi, the Jewish underground military organization fighting for the Jewish State against the British and, after their departure, against the invading Arab armies.

Little did my parents know what lay in store for us. My

mother only felt that there was the greatest danger, but Eli knew. He pointed at the twin posters in Russian with the caption Y HNX (On Their Side, that is, the capitalist countries) showing bombs raining from the sky, burning buildings, women fleeing through the flames and smoke, and Y HAC (On Our Side) showing a woman carrying a smiling baby and red fighter planes flying above assuring their security. Eli predicted that very soon they would be able to take off the one with the mother and baby and write Y HNX N Y HAC on the one showing the war.

In the middle of June 1941, all the formerly rich Jews and non-Jews, owners of shops, factories and real estate, were rounded up and deported to Siberia as 'Enemies of the Working Class'. Their properties had been confiscated before – 'nationalized' the procedure was called – and now they were being loaded on the trains allowed to take one suitcase each. Doctors, lawyers, engineers and other members of free professions, were left alone. Of the Gudin family, only the son was left; and he continued to come to our house in order to observe the treatment of varicose veins. My mother wanted to go to the railway station to say goodbye to his father who had been allowed to phone before he was taken away, but she was forbidden to leave the house. It was all right for the young doctor Gudin to come for medical studies, but to be seen bidding farewell to an exploiter of the working class might result in our own deportation.

Many projects were planned while strolling through Stalino Prospectas, the former Avenue of Liberty, or sitting on benches in the Kovno Opera Park; and although many acquaintances were missing, nobody really worried even about relatives. As one Russian song had it, '. . . Siberia is also Russian soil'. Those who had been taken away could not be really so badly off within the bosom of Mother Russia.

I had finished elementary school, and now it was time to consider my future education. The school authorities had recommended that I be sent to Moscow to enter the preparatory school for political commissars. My brother was to be sent to the Crimea to spend the summer because of his frail constitution.

The prospect of getting to wear a uniform was attractive. Yet going to Moscow would frustrate any chance of escaping to Palestine. Such possibilities still existed; but being under-age, I had no passport of my own and therefore could not even try to get away. However, others had made their way out via Japan. During the second half of 1940, Sampo Sugihara, the Japanese Consul in Kovno, had issued 3,500 Japanese visas as a humanitarian gesture, without any formalities.[16]

Many times during those long warm summer evenings, my mother begged to be allowed to go and see the Japanese Consul, who lived only a few houses from us, about a visa; but my father did not allow it. What if any of the Russian officers living on the fourth floor saw her entering the Consulate? Did she want us all to be sent to Siberia? And who did she think she was that the Consul of Japan would see her? She didn't even know how to speak proper German, so how was she going to talk Japanese?

She certainly could not speak Japanese, but she had her premonitions. Just as her mother before her had left everything and had taken only her two children in the opening stages of the First World War, so my mother wanted to save our lives because she sensed the great danger. However, she was unable to muster the arguments needed to persuade her husband. His ridicule, the humiliations, his threats, were too much to bear. All she could do was hold my brother close to her and soothe his crying, because of the inevitable argument that would break out.

WAR

It was in the early morning of June 22, 1941, when air-raid warnings were sounded following the German invasion of Russia. The heavy curtains were drawn. Total darkness filled the room as the sirens started howling. I was shivering. Minutes later, heavy explosions shook the building.

Fearing to put the light on, I pulled the curtains apart to let in the grey, early morning light. Our alarm clock showed a quarter past four. Teeth chattering, I quickly dressed while my mother busied herself with my brother.

I had never had a Bar Mitzvah (the ceremony initiating Jewish boys to religious duty and responsibilities at the age of thirteen). A month earlier, on my thirteenth birthday, a few friends had come to my house to celebrate, all wearing the obligatory red scarf. I remembered this as the sirens started again, thinking that I might not live to have another birthday. I tied my red scarf tightly around my neck, as if donning a shield, to protect me from my fear.

Should I pray? I wondered what my father had done with the yarmulke.

Should I go and look for Zelda?

Nonsense!

I ran down the stairs with everyone else to hide in the cellar, but it was too late. The stairs leading there were blocked by others who had come before us. Since no explosions could be heard, I went out into the street.

A gust of wind, followed by another explosion, threw me to the wall. It became dark – I looked for flames but saw only heavy smoke growing into one black cloud above the houses.

A truck arrived and stopped in front of our entrance. Almost immediately, the colonel who lived on the fourth floor appeared with his wife and his sons, all carrying suitcases, rushing up again, returning with blankets, a radio . . .

'Can we come with you?' my mother asked, mixing Russian and Polish.

'Get in the truck and let's go!' the colonel shouted back.

We climbed onto the truck while the colonel held out his hand to help my mother.

'Get down immediately!' my father roared.

My mother tried to persuade him to go but to no avail.

'Doctor, come with us. The Germans will kill you!' the colonel tried to intervene. However, embarrassed by father's behaviour, he helped my brother down off the truck. When I made no move to get down, my father climbed up, grabbed me by my hair, dragged me to the edge and pushed me so that I was forced to jump.

The truck left, the Russians waved goodbye and we returned to our flat – to the paintings, the Persian carpets, and the mental comfort provided by the German-Jewish middle class, which outweighed the clear Jewish head and common sense of my mother. We sat in the kitchen, eating hard-boiled eggs and drinking tea. There were more explosions, but we were not allowed to go down again.

My father was worried about Mrs Serebrowicz. He called her up.

'No, no, there is nothing to worry about. We are German citizens. I am sure that they will need doctors, too,' he assured her. I did not hear what she said in reply, but they went on talking for quite a while until another explosion caused a strong draught, and the conversation came to an end.

My father told us that Mr Serebrowicz had been released from prison, that he would come to visit us soon, and he warned us to stay inside, to lock the door and not to open it to anyone. Not to go out either, because the Lithuanians were beating up Jews in the streets. My mother ran to lock the door. My father tried for hours to get Berlin on the radio, but only crackling sounds emerged from the same old box on which we had heard Hitler's voice back home in Innsbruck.

We heard shots outside. Lithuanians were shooting at retreating Russian soldiers who were dragging themselves through the streets, abandoning their guns by throwing them on carts drawn by horses exhausted and collapsing under the load.

Darkness fell, and we went to bed without taking off our clothes. The bombardments stopped. Throughout the following day, shots could still be heard outside, but I was not allowed near the window.

Wearing a scarf, my mother sat in the kitchen reading 'Tehilim' (psalms) from a prayer book. I was still wearing the red scarf I had put on the day before. My father entered the kitchen and suddenly tore off the red-enamelled clasp, ripped the scarf into pieces, lifted some garbage from the bin, and covered the scarf and clasp with some potato peels. Another uniform was gone.

Shooting continued through the night. Again, we went to bed in our clothes, leaving the windows open to prevent the panes from breaking by bursts of air pressure following explosions. We could not sleep because the voices of drunks roaming the streets, mingled at times with the shrieks of women, continued till morning. The second day of the war was over. We found out from listening to the radio that the Germans had come. A voice announced: 'Achtung! Achtung! Es wird gewarnt! Fuer jeden verwundeten deutschen Soldaten werden hundert Juden erschossen! Wir wiederholen . . . (Attention! Attention! For every wounded German soldier, one hundred Jews will be shot! We repeat . . .)'

Then it was broadcast in Lithuanian.

My brother and I were sitting on the bedroom floor playing with cut-out coloured paper soldiers, when my father called from his study.

'Ernst, come here!'

'What for?'

'I said, come here!'

I crossed the corridor to find him staring into the yellow light of the radio while the voice continued in Lithuanian.

'Translate!'

'It's the same as in German.'

'Translate, you dirty dog,' he roared at the top of his voice, while tears ran down my mother's face.

Slowly, I started translating as the radio repeated the message every fifteen minutes, interrupted by German military music.

'Attention! Attention! Jews have been shooting at German soldiers. We warn you! For every wounded German soldier . . .'

I was choking on my tears. Then he hit me. Over and over again, slapping me in the face using both the palm and the back of his hand.

Ever since then, and despite the fact that I have a perfect command of several languages, I am unable to translate without tremendous fear. When asked by my employer a few years ago to translate a German document, my vehement refusal caused my eventual dismissal under a different pretext. While he was explaining the importance of the deal to me, all I could see was my father slapping me while the warning 'Achtung! Achtung!' resounded in my ears.

The reader will I hope forgive these digressions from the narrative; but in order to prevent generalizations, it must be shown that there are no closed chapters in the lives of individuals and that there can therefore be no pasts forgotten or forgiven.

Mr Serebrowicz phoned to ask my father to come to his house on some urgent matter. My father's apprehension, caused by the repeated radio broadcast and the single shots which could still be heard, was assuaged by Mr Serebrowicz's promise to send a German soldier as an escort. My father gathered his instruments, carefully choosing new syringes – he had not been told what urgent work was to be done. We had run out of food, so my mother asked him to borrow a few eggs and a loaf of bread from Mrs Serebrowicz for the children. She got no reply.

The doorbell rang, and she went to answer it. A German soldier, wearing the black collar tabs of the Waffen SS and carrying a gun strapped over his shoulder, stood outside. In the most polite manner usually reserved for patients, the soldier was invited to come in.

He bellowed, 'Doktor Haber?'

'Ich komme sofort (I'm coming immediately),' my father replied and, carrying his instrument pouch, left with the soldier.

We watched from the window and saw the German order him into the gutter, where he continued to march until he disappeared around the corner, followed by the German who walked on the sidewalk a few paces behind.

He came back very late. Again, the German was invited in but he refused. We went into the kitchen, and my father started taking food from a huge basket he had brought with him. Eggs, a huge loaf of brown bread, some apples and a thick slab of lard which reeked like the pungent smell of butcheries.

'But this is treife (ritually unclean, forbidden food)!' my mother cried.

'This is pikuach nefesh (relaxing the Jewish law to save a life)!' he retorted.

'I never heard of Jews eating pork because of pikuach nefesh.'

'I am the doctor. And when a doctor prescribes pork because of pikuach nefesh, it is pikuach nefesh!'

'Your mother should hear you!'

'Leave my mother out of this!'

'Did Mrs Serebrowicz send this?'

'Now shut up and prepare some dinner. You have to cut the lard into very fine slices.'

Hungry as I was, I could not bite into the fatty white slice of lard, gleaming with moisture, spread on the piece of bread he handed to me. In Spain, the Jews had been given the choice to eat pork or be killed, and they had chosen to be killed. Nobody had told us that if we did not eat pork,

48

we would be killed. We could eat dry bread to satisfy our hunger.

I nearly vomited. My father glared at me, my mother covered her face, screaming, 'Vei is mir! (Woe is me)!' I ran into the bedroom, but my father followed me with the lard and did not let go of me until I bit into the greasy evil-smelling piece of fat.

'Pikuach nefesh' . . . The logical sequence to the abolition of the Superior Policeman became justification for every moral turpitude then, and later, during the 1950s and '60s in the State of Israel, the term 'pikuach nefesh' was used to justify the actions of the European Jewish leaders and to cover up their role in the destruction of their own people. The cover-up is well described by Hanna Ahrendt:

> That the prosecution in Jerusalem, so careful not to embarrass the Adenauer administration, should have avoided, with even greater and more obvious justification, bringing this chapter of the story into the open was almost a matter of course.[17]

Life returned to normal; we had settled into a certain routine. A few Lithuanian patients appeared again in the waiting room, and it happened quite often that butter, eggs or other items of food were offered in payment. In the afternoon, the German soldier came to escort my father on necessary house-calls, after which he took him to Mr Serebrowicz – returning him late at night.

Because I was not allowed onto the street, I used to settle myself in the dining room with a book, interrupting my reading only for meals in the kitchen. My brother played in the bedroom with his teddy bear as if it were a live companion. I warned him to stay away from me because I wanted quiet. Immersed in the literary works of Greek and German mythology with which our library abounded, I lived in a world of heroes, lovers and beautiful women for whom men made great sacrifices for reasons I could not understand. Yet, I was always alert to what I might hear from behind the sliding door. I went to the keyhole whenever I noticed somebody who, judging from his or her looks, seemed exceptional – anybody I suspected of having come for reasons other than medical treatment.

The rumours started spreading among quite a number of people about the Jewish doctor from Germany who was being escorted by a soldier of the Waffen SS on house-calls and then to Mr Serebrowicz. The fact that Mr Serebrowicz and Dr Haber had been seen a number of times entering the Gestapo headquarters indicated that they had become very influential. It was still not clear to me what they were doing at the Gestapo.

GOOD CONNECTIONS

The first petitioner was Mrs Levy. She had heard about the doctor's good connections with the German authorities and came to seek his help. Her husband had been shot a week earlier when the Lithuanians were roaming the streets killing Jews. A German sergeant to whom she had appealed for help agreed to move into the flat with her until things calmed down a bit. When she addressed him in broken German, he recognized her English accent; and, assuming she was not Jewish, he did not mind living with her. However, he had a change of heart and left her.

She was hoping that my father could get the Germans to understand that with a British passport and not being Jewish, she was entitled to some protection now that she was all alone and penniless. 'Maybe they are gentlemen after all.'

To alleviate her financial difficulties, Mrs Levy was engaged to teach us English. Since we were not allowed to go to school, it had been decided that we could not while away our time without learning something. And Mrs Levy needed the money. She taught us by speaking only English, explaining herself slowly, and having us look up the words in the dictionary. Even my mother joined us. The English vowels; the 'th' which was not 's' but 'the'; repeating 'the' while having us look into her mouth to show us how to run the tongue backwards on the palate to get the sound right. After lessons were over, she would stay for a chat and have a cup of tea. She could not explain why in English one says 'to have a cup of tea' and not 'to drink one'. As she painstakingly tried to answer our questions, she started to form German sentences much sooner than we were able to grasp such complicated meanings as 'not really' which meant neither 'no' nor 'yes'.

While spending a vacation in Paris away from Sarawak, in the British East Indies, where her first husband was a very important person in the government, she had met Mr Levy, fallen in love with him, and followed him to Lithuania. It had taken a long time until her divorce came through; but eventually they were married in a civil ceremony, so there was no need for her to become Jewish. They had been very happy together.

Most of all, Mrs Levy missed the animals she had left behind in Sarawak. She had even had her own tiger which was kept in a cage. Lovely birds abounded in the garden surrounding their mansion. One day, she brought us pictures, one of which showed her in an open carriage drawn by two black horses. She was seated next to an officer wearing a plumed hat with a splendid uniform covered with medals. Only the climate, the terrible heat and humidity, did not agree with her. That was why every summer she would travel to Europe – mostly to the continent, to Rome, to Paris – where one could meet so many interesting people.

It was a good thing, though, that with Mr Levy now dead, she could still support herself with English lessons. 'It was really very generous of Dr Haber,' she said and dabbed her eyes with her handkerchief.

Then one day she was gone. She had followed the doctor's advice and gone to see a high-ranking officer at the Gestapo, who had promised to look into the matter so that she would not have to move into the Ghetto together with the Jews. But she never returned from there. My father asked Mr Serebrowicz if he knew anything. After a few days, he was told that they had shot Mrs Levy because she was an English spy.

Next were Mr Teitelman and his visibly pregnant wife who came to seek my father's intervention. They were both American citizens and did not think they had to move into the Ghetto. The Lithuanians had beaten him up because of his beard and peies (sidelocks); but the moment he had shown them his passport, which he always carried with him, they let him go. He had come to Lithuania to learn at the Slobodka Yeshiva. A suitable match was arranged and he got married. Although the Bolsheviks had come the

52

year before, he did not return home because his wife was reluctant to leave her family. Now that both her mother and her father had been killed by the Lithuanians, she wanted to go to America. Before the Russians came to Lithuania, Mr Teitelman saw to it that her name and picture were added to his passport.

My father remarked that America was a neutral country, and he was sure the Germans would allow them to travel to Berlin to see the American Ambassador. He promised them that they would get the necessary papers. When they went to the Gestapo to get the papers, they were arrested. Mr Serebrowicz explained that they were shot because the Germans had no time for such nonsense as sending 'yeshiva bochers' back to America when there was a war on.

'AKTION'

Karl Jaeger, Chief of the Gestapo in Kovno, had asked Serebrowicz to prepare a list of educated Jews – including doctors, engineers, lawyers – who could be useful to the war effort, adding to each name the home address, a short account of professional qualifications, and property owned.

Because Serebrowicz's knowledge of German was very rudimentary, he introduced 'Der Doktor' (as he used to call my father) to Standartenfuehrer (Colonel) Jaeger and took him along as his interpreter to meetings with the Gestapo chief or with lower-ranking officers. During one of these meetings, my father showed them recommendations from high-ranking Lithuanian officals who were either patients themselves or friends of the former prime minister. They certified that his transfer to the Ghetto would be most detrimental to people undergoing treatment and that a postponement of at least a year was required. A Lithuanian physician with whom my father kept close relations also certified to this fact. Mr Serebrowicz seconded the recommendation, with the result that my father received an official permit allowing us to live outside the Ghetto and exempting us from wearing the Yellow Star (Star of David cut from yellow material, about four inches in diameter, sewn on the front and back of every garment). He was now free to move without an escort.

To prepare the required list, they decided to use my father's study in order to avoid being interrupted by all sorts of petitioners who came to Serebrowicz's house. Since the work could be started only after consultation hours, Mrs Serebrowicz offered to bring some food; and, together with my mother, prepared a very nice dinner – 'just like before the war'.

After extensive discussion over who to include on the list and whom to leave out, my father composed a memorandum praising the achievements of the persons listed and their absolute allegiance to the German authorities. Many of the persons listed had obtained degrees from German universities and could thus be relied upon not to betray their 'cultural heritage'.

The memorandum was read aloud at the dinner table, and Mrs Serebrowicz praised the beautiful language while my mother looked down as if the matter did not concern her. At first, she had refused to go along with the idea of the dinner. She also had not shared her husband's enthusiasm about not moving into the Ghetto like everyone else. Hearing about 'our common German cultural heritage', she looked at me as if she wanted to ask me – did you hear that?! Is he out of his mind? But although I felt uneasy myself, I did not really understand why. My attention was directed towards Yardena Serebrowicz, who had come along with her sister Carmela to have dinner with us. She was fourteen and Carmela was sixteen. Yardena seemed much bigger than I at the time. They didn't say a word, except that Yardena offered to take me to the cinema one day, seeing that they were operating again and that we were allowed to move about without wearing the 'stars'.

A few days after the dinner, while the 'intellectuals' were being rounded up, Yardena and I went to see a German movie about the bombing of Warsaw and the victory in Poland. I was glad that I hadn't been there. My brother did not want to come with us; he wanted to stay with mother. When I returned home, my mother looked at me in silence, as if I had done something wrong. When Yardena said goodbye, she closed the door behind her without a word.

I was never allowed to go out again. My black hair would draw attention, and one shouldn't draw attention. The Serebrowicz girls looked Jewish too. The permit was always with my father, which he needed to see his patients and Mr Serebrowicz, whom he visited almost daily. He always spoke of lists, of valuables transferred from the Ghetto to the Germans and about the riches Mr Serebrowicz was amassing.

Only once more was I allowed to go down as far as the courtyard. A column of Jewish workers had halted in front of our house, when a few of them broke ranks to rummage through the garbage bins. I called my mother to the window, and she quickly wrapped a loaf of bread, a slab of butter and some potatoes in an old newspaper and told me to go down and give it to one of them. They asked me if I was Jewish, but I ran up the stairs again without answering. It was forbidden to talk to Jews. My mother had warned me not to say a word and not to tell 'Dem Vater' (she always used the definite article when speaking about him).

Whenever she mentioned Serebrowicz, she always said 'Herr' before his name, although he never addressed her directly. He never looked at anybody. His eyes were continuously shifting as if he were looking for something or afraid somebody might suddenly appear and kill him.

He took to wearing German officer's boots, a black leather overcoat which he always removed after putting his gun on the table next to where he would sit down. Golden teeth glittered in his mouth: he resembled a Negro with his curly hair and heavy lips. I was sure that Mrs Serebrowicz had married him for his money. He never said hello or goodbye to anyone. Whenever he entered our house, my mother became very ill-at-ease and closed herself up in the kitchen with my brother. As usual, I took my place in the dining room from where I could hear every word they said, observing them occasionally through the keyhole.

On October 26, 1941, he came in the morning. My mother was told not to show anybody in and to tell patients that the doctor was not at home. Again, they were to prepare a list which Helmut Rauca, the Gestapo officer in charge of the Kovno Ghetto needed urgently. The Aeltestenrat (Council of Elders heading the Jewish administration of the Ghetto) had sent the list for submission to the Gestapo. It contained the names of all 'indispensable' persons. Mr Serebrowicz was now adding names of persons he wanted to be classified as 'indispensable' by deleting names of persons he either did not know or whom he found 'dispensable'. My father wrote out the names of Serebrowicz's candidates in German and made recommendations of his own. The argument arose whether men of education or persons of property should be preferred. Although educated people were more valuable, it was finally decided that considering the vast amounts of money that had been offered for inclusion in the list, the 'prize' would go to the highest bidder. At the beginning, I did not quite understand the meaning of the discussion; but when, one late afternoon, only family names and amounts of dollars, rubles or pieces of gold were read out, I understood that this time the meeting was very important.

My father completed the last of his recommendations, reading them out loud and emphasizing the importance of the person's work in support of the German armed forces. During the whole process, Mr Serebrowicz was very agitated and raised his voice every now and then, calling one or another man an idiot or thief. But as I understood it, he was nervous because he was in a hurry to finish the job. Rauca had asked him to go to Vilna on an important mission. It was very late at night when he finally left our house.

The next morning, my father ordered the door locked, complete silence to be observed, and nobody to open the door no matter what. The telephone was not to be answered.

An 'Aktion' (mass killing operation) was planned for the next day in the Ghetto. Ten thousand people were to be evacuated, but we had nothing to fear. Rauca had assured my father that neither our family nor Mrs Serebrowicz would be evacuated while her husband was in Vilna for two days. Anyway, only people who were unable to work were affected by the order, and, of course, all those whose names were on the 'Aeltestenrat' list were exempt. Rauca had even accepted my father's invitation to have dinner with us and the Serebrowicz's. But one could not be sure. They had also promised Mr Teitelman a permit to go to Berlin.

The door was locked in order to make the authorities think that we were already gone, in case some German administrative branch, other than the 'Sicherheitsdienst' (Security Service of the SS) to which Rauca belonged, decided to arrest us and confiscate our belongings. Many Jews suffered because of conflicting interests among various German authorities. Each of us hid in a different room as if the very sight of another person could be dangerous. Only my brother kept by his mother in the kitchen.

My father rested on the couch in his study. With the help of a dictionary, I tried to read *Gone With the Wind* which Mrs Levy had left us as a present. My mother told us not to eat, because she said that her father had always fasted when there was great danger during the First World War. However, when my brother started crying because he was hungry, she gave him some bread. My father entered the kitchen and declared that fasting was nonsense. In the end, only my mother fasted.

At night, we were sent to bed and warned not to take our clothes off. It must have been very late when I was awakened by a terrible shriek. At first, I thought some drunks were chasing women; but as I woke up completely, I realized that it was my mother. I got up and went into the consultation room. I saw my father, with a syringe in his hand, pulling my mother towards the couch.

'Ernst, he wants to kill us! Vai is mir! He wants to kill us!'

My brother was clinging to her free hand and trying to

pull her in the other direction. I shouted at my father to stop and raised my knife which I had opened when I heard my mother's shriek. When he saw me coming with the knife, he let go of my mother and put down the syringe.

'I thought it would be better if I did it before they came to get us,' he said to no one in particular.

'Then do it to yourself,' I shouted. 'And leave her alone. You can go up to the fourth floor and jump into the street like Mrs Goldenberg.'

He sat down on the couch and stared in front of him. After a while, my mother told us to go back to our room. I left immediately and my brother came a few minutes later, telling me that they had gone to sleep. Not daring to fall asleep, we sat on the floor playing checkers until morning. When my mother came to call us for breakfast, we saw that she had been crying.

We did not see our father again until the evening, when he came into the kitchen to tell my mother that it was getting late. He was dressed in his best suit. I was to set the table in the dining room for five persons. Mr and Mrs Serebrowicz were to sit on one side, my parents on the other, and Herr Rauca at the head of the table. I carefully laid out the plates and the Yontefdikeh silver, normally reserved for holidays.

My mother called from the kitchen to my father, 'If he sees the silver, he'll take it. You forgot we had to hand it over?'

'Then hide it again.'

Within seconds, my mother took the silver from the table. I had to start all over again. Knife and spoon on the right; fork on the left. It reminded me of the Seder when he had hit her because of the salt. I placed the salt right next to Rauca's place.

As soon as I had finished, there was a knock at the door. Yardena and Carmela had stayed at home. Rauca smelled of sweat. He immediately unbuckled his belt with the gun, took off his overcoat and his uniform jacket and threw them all over an empty chair. He sat down at the head of the table in his armsleeves with his garters showing. My mother had not changed for the occasion. It was no Yontef for her. The contrast between the German without his jacket and his two Jewish assistants all dressed up and Mrs Serebrowicz looking her very best spoiled the festivity my father had wanted to lend to the occasion. There were even candles on the table, but nobody had lit them.

'So, nun machen wir's uns schoen gemuetlich, (Now, let's get nice and comfortable),' said Rauca and everybody took their seats. He had come straight from the Ninth Fort (one of several fortifications only a few miles outside the town) where Jews were being executed. On that evening of October 28, 1941, and continuing throughout the next day, about ten thousand people were taken from the Kovno Ghetto to the Ninth Fort and shot. Rauca commanded and supervized the Aktion, both at the point of selection in the Ghetto and later at the point of execution at the fort.

It was not until one year later that my brother and I learned what had happened at the fort that very same evening that Rauca was dining with our parents and the Serebrowicz's. But by that time, we had already become accustomed to eating and reading while others were being killed. As long as it was not *us*. As time went on, the *us* turned into *me*, except for my mother who until her last day only thought of *us*.

Rauca's visit had increased our sense of security. Even though Jews continued to be shot at the Ninth Fort, as we found out from veiled remarks made during Mr Serebrowicz's visits, the shootings could have taken place on the moon as far as we were concerned. Patients were treated, afternoon naps were taken. There was no shortage of food, and we followed the events of the war through the pages of the daily papers and the German army illustrated weekly *Signal*. The radio had been given to a neighbour for safekeeping until after the war, but once a week my father would read us Goebbels' editorial in *Das Reich*, the leading German weekly. Under the guise of wishing to keep us still better informed, he read to us aloud in the impeccable German he was so proud of. But we felt that he was trying to reiterate that we still belonged to them, the Germans, whose 'cultural heritage' we shared, in spite of the fear of what they might do to us, and the fact that he himself had nearly killed us. Because we had been left out, he thought this proved that they had taken our German citizenship into consideration. And, after all, the liquidation of the Jews was part of the excesses brought about by the war. Once it was over, Germany would return to its cultural splendour, the spirit of Schiller and Goethe, the beauty of Mozart and Beethoven.

Today too, when Jews are being killed, life continues as if acts of terror were unavoidable natural occurrences. Reading editorials out aloud to one's family has gone out of fashion, but television provides a continuous run of statements and speeches by leading terrorists. Although they lack the authority of the German minister of propaganda, they lack none of the fascination to those Israelis who interview, quote and thereby almost justify them, much in the same manner as my father explained German policy by quoting Dr Joseph Goebbels.

THE GHETTO

Our expulsion order to the Kovno Ghetto coincided with the German victories in southern Russia during August 1942. My father, who had prophesied that with German victories their hatred of the Jews would subside, was perplexed when Mr Serebrowicz came to announce that he had been transferred to Vilna and that we had to move into the Ghetto. Arrangements had already been made for us to receive decent lodgings and for the continuation of the treatment of Lithuanian patients at a house just inside the Ghetto gate.

The Serebrowicz family spent the last night before their departure at our house. A flat was waiting for them in Vilna – not in the Ghetto of course – and everyone was looking forward to a new life. When they arrived in Vilna, they were taken from the train straight to the Gestapo headquarters and shot.

Three days later, we moved into the Ghetto. Most of our belongings had to be left behind; only beds, blankets, some kitchenware, and a few chairs were loaded on a horse-drawn cart which the Gestapo had sent together with a guard. The night before, my mother sewed yellow stars on all our jackets. Neighbours stood in the street watching as we set out on our way following the cart, with the guard behind us, his gun over his shoulder.

When we arrived at the Ghetto gate, Captain Gudin of the Jewish Ghetto police was waiting for us. The insignia of rank on his dark blue visored cap, the brassard with the

Star of David and the shining black boots gave the man an air of competence and authority. The gate was swung wide open and after a perfunctory search, Mr Gudin led us to our lodgings from which the former residents had been 'evacuated'.

When the beds, the Chair, and our kitchen table were carried in, there was practically no room left to move about. A carpenter arrived the same day and put the beds together, one on top of the other, thus leaving some space in each of the two rooms. A small porch was enclosed with boards, leaving an opening fitted with a pane of glass, to become a kitchen.

The universal respect with which doctors were regarded brought them to prominence and inspired confidence in those who depended on them. It was no coincidence that until the last days of the Ghetto, the Germans supported Dr Elhanan Elkes, the Chairman of the Council of Elders, who could be relied upon in every respect and be trusted to look after his own. The following two passages from the diary of the Secretary of the Council of Elders will illustrate those attitudes:

Dr Elkes listened gravely to Stutz, the SS Oberschar-fuehrer who replaced Rauca in mid-1942 as the Gestapo officer in charge of the Ghetto. He saw before him not a cruel Nazi leader but a sick human being who was asking him for medical assistance. The doctor was in a quandary both as a Jew and the head of the Jewish community in the Ghetto and as a physician. However, the conflict did not last long. In the end, his medical 'ethics' won out. Dr Elkes diagnosed the illness and wrote a prescription.[18]

During the selection of the 10,000 Jews to be shot at Ninth Fort on October 28 and 29, Dr Elkes attempted to save, and at times, he succeeded, in passing a whole family to the left side. He was seen interceding for a veteran public personality, a head of a hospital department or a good craftsman. He even tried to improve the lot of a number of Zionist and non-Zionist functionaries and others.[19]

Dr Haber fell into the same category. After having spent one year 'outside', nobody suspected and nobody reported his activities in association with Serebrowicz. His past and continuing privileges were consequently attributed to his special medical skills. The fact that he was allowed to continue receiving patients from the 'outside' enhanced his professional and personal standing. When the Gestapo withdrew permission for him to treat Lithuanians, the Council immediately integrated him into the Ghetto medical service. Illness certificates signed by him allowed people to be exempted from labour duty. Both the Jewish Labour Office and the German authorities were confident that his decisions were strictly medical and that dispensations were accorded only in cases of extreme illness. Illness caused by undernourishment was no justification for granting an exemption.

Because his rigid professionalism was so highly regarded by the Aeltestenrat, Mr Lipcer, who succeeded Serebrowicz as intermediary between the Council of Elders and the Gestapo and was the Ghetto's most feared personality, made my father his family's personal physician – a position equal to the one my father had enjoyed as physician to the Prime Minister of Lithuania.

We became Dr Haber's sons. His fame and position had turned us into the offspring of a public figure, putting a distance between us and other boys our age. My mother hid in anonymity and started the quest for food, which, in spite of my father's position, had become scarce.

Sometimes, at the risk of her life, she would approach the Ghetto fence near our house and trade a silver spoon for a loaf of bread or a slab of butter. But when my father threatened to denounce her, she stopped. In his position, he could not afford to have her caught smuggling food into the Ghetto. She continued trading what remained of our valuables with Jewish middlemen, but she received only half of what she would have got at the fence.

In order to ensure strict justice within the family, our daily bread ration was distributed by lottery. The two prizes were the ends of the loaf, because they were harder to chew and therefore lasted longer. Each day someone else would turn his back to the table where my mother placed the carefully sliced loaf. My father would point at random to one of the slices and ask: 'For whom?'

'For mother.'

Since only working people were entitled to bread, it was very generous of my father to allow the ration to be divided among the four of us. He became angry every time he thought the loaf had not been sliced 'exactly' into four equal portions – allowing for the end pieces to be slightly thinner considering that they lasted longer. I always wondered why he didn't do the slicing himself. However, being the only one in the family who was working, he made the laws.

In those days, to be working was almost a sure guarantee against being included in a transport to death. 'As long as they need us, they won't kill us.' That was the official line of the Council of Elders, and that was confirmed by German officials with whom contacts were kept at every level. In reality, however, the Council knew that this was not the case. 'Ponar [where 5000 Jews from Vilna were shot] taught us once more, that not the work for the Germans, not the slavery and the submission, will help us when our turn will come.'[20] Yet, this knowledge did not deter the Council from accepting and submitting to German policies.

Having entered the Ghetto vocational training centre as a locksmith apprentice, I soon adopted the philosophy that only those fit for work were useful and, therefore, entitled to live. Life became the remuneration for work performed in the service of the Germans.

As 'Dr Haber's son', I was received with suspicious curiosity when I arrived at the vocational school. The fact that we had been allowed by the Germans to live 'outside' for a whole year, coupled with the important position that my father held in the Ghetto medical service, created an unsurmountable barrier despite my efforts at being sociable.

The fact that I wore glasses and woollen gloves brought me the nickname 'the intelligent locksmith'. My short-sightedness had been diagnosed by my father, and he used his connections to obtain glasses from the 'outside' according to a prescription made in the Ghetto. I needed the woollen gloves because of frostbite that I had contracted while handling metal in the open air during the winter.

To avoid being hurt by the ridicule, I concentrated on the quality of my work. I did not allow myself to make the slightest error. I meticulously filed and polished every piece of metal, thoroughly oiling every moving part of every mechanism. Special jobs came my way. When my mother

66

moved the kitchen stove into our combined bedroom and dining room to provide more heat, I turned the porch into a workshop using the tools I had stolen from school.

Stealing came as easily as lying. I explained to my father that someone had lent me the tools to do small jobs after working hours. Had I been caught, I would have said that I had taken them only for a day or two and planned to return them later.

People needed locks to be repaired, engraved initials to be removed from silver cutlery, keys to be fitted. Payment was to be made in advance in Russian rubles. Stalingrad had turned the ruble into hard currency again. I piled one ten-ruble note upon another and hid them in an iron box beneath the roof, accessible through a well-disguised opening in the ceiling. If the occasion should arise for me to run away, the money would come in handy.

I thought about escape but made no real plans, because I had already immersed myself into furthering my 'career' at school, which had been turned into a regular workshop.

We received an order for 80,000 soldiers' identification tags. A metal stamping press was installed to be manually operated by three workers, and I was put in charge. I shouted in German whenever the men tried to rest from swinging the heavy rotary fly wheel which drove down the stamping shaft. Daily production was increased and faulty discs rejected to the satisfaction of the management, and the Germans, who ordered another 80,000.

I no longer received my ration of bread as a favour from my father. I ate and lived in my own right. I still wore gloves and glasses, but now I was a Vorarbeiter (foreman), and the German title brought respect. My fellow workers laughed only behind my back.

The workshop had three departments: a metal shop, a carpentry shop for boys aged between fourteen and sixteen and a sewing shop for girls of the same ages. After working hours, boys and girls congregated in small groups on the staircases and empty floors of the unfinished building. They used to go home for dinner and come back later at night, turning the place into a social club. The wind blew through the windowless spaces and only the staircases leading to the locked cellars provided some protection from the weather. As there was no light of any kind, meetings took place only when moonlight broke the darkness.

Having become stand-offish due to my position, I shunned these meetings to avoid contacts with my fellow workers or 'the girls from upstairs' as the seamstresses were called.

One day, I was sent to the first floor to check a sewing machine which had become stuck. The operator kept watching me as I was cleaning and oiling the machine, and suddenly I remembered that at school before the war, she had shared a desk with Zelda. She had grown taller, and instead of pigtails she now wore her hair parted in the middle, falling down straight on both sides of her face which was dominated by large blue eyes. Her name was Yoheved.

'Did you know that they shot Zelda?' she asked.

I was unable to say a word. The sudden realization that my last emotional refuge had been given a physical dimension and had been destroyed at the same time paralyzed me completely. The fact that the question was asked in Hebrew threw me back into a world which I had completely forgotten. I must have turned white. She picked up the screwdriver which had fallen from my hand and asked, 'What's the matter?'

'Nothing,' was all I could say, and I left.

She overtook me on my way home. Carefully avoiding physical contact as I walked at her side, she told me that the day the Germans came, Zelda had wanted to try and get some milk for her cat. When Zelda went into the street, one of her neighbours shot and killed her.

While Yoheved was talking, I recalled Zelda's face; and although I had just been told that she was dead, I saw her in her light blue woollen cap, walking beside me through the snow on our way home from school.

Tears ran down my face.

ZIONISM

It became routine for Yoheved and I to walk home together from work. Not having any future, we talked mostly about childhood memories and food. The youthful habit of building castles in the air was hampered by the constant gnawing of hunger, allowing only fantasies of delicacies which would be consumed 'once the war was over'.

Yoheved kept accusing me of being too proud for refusing to join her with the others at the nightly social gatherings, so I finally gave in.

I could not clearly distinguish faces in the darkness at first, but gradually I became accustomed to it, voices helping to identify the members of the various little groups. I did not have to ask my way, because the moment I arrived, someone told me that Yoheved was on the second floor. I realized that we were now considered a 'couple'. Apart from Yoheved, there were two other girls and a carpenter who had formed a close circle on the landing of the staircase.

'Here comes the intellectual locksmith,' they greeted me, and immediately I regretted having come. As I turned to go, one of the girls grabbed me. They wanted me to tell them my plans for the future. Each of them had already told their plans – or dreams as they actually were. Yoheved had told them how educated I was, so they wanted to know my intentions too. Each of them briefly repeated their 'dreams'.

The carpenter was going to go to America where he had an uncle. One of the girls was going to wait for the Red Army, who would punish the Germans and the Lithuanians. Yoheved and the other girl vowed to go to Palestine. Only in Palestine could Jews live freely without having to be afraid of anyone. They were going to live in a Jewish State, where nobody would be able to harm them. Annoyed by what I considered to be nonsensical daydreaming, I blurted out:

'I am going to go as far away as possible from Jews!'

'What?!'

The consternation was complete. Even though I could not read their faces in the dark, their common exclamation made it clear to me that I had said the wrong thing. Yoheved tried to help me out, but I had already embarked upon my course.

I explained that a Jewish State would be run in much the same manner as the Ghetto. Take away the Germans and you have a Jewish State. No need to travel all the way to Palestine. The words landed like a bombshell, especially coming from a former Betari. Yet, as I expanded my theory, they were as dumbfounded by my arguments as they had been aroused by my statement. Being surrounded by Arabs, there would always be a fence around the country; and if one would try to cross the fence, one would be shot. The Jewish State would develop favouritism and corruption on every level of society just as rampant as in the Ghetto – with queues for bread and medical attention and work, and other queues for those who did not have to queue because of their good connections with the various members of the Aeltestenrat. Jewish policemen? At the gate, they were sometimes worse than the Germans. So what is the basis for believing that in the State of the Jews, policemen would be any different? To avoid the possibility of eventually falling into their hands – if I came out alive – I told them that I would go to Australia where nobody knew me and where I didn't know anybody and where there were no Jews.

Of all those who were present that night on the stairs of the vocational training centre, I was the only one to survive and to realize both their dreams and mine. My 1943 appraisal of Australia proved to be wrong. It was neither free of competing and feuding Jewish communities – each looking after their own – nor of perpetually drunken gentiles who, in their majority, considered their Jewish countrymen as the Lithuanians had considered theirs.

Having arrived there in 1964 on a business assignment from the rough and tumble and rather drab young State of Israel which was devoid of European culture and behaviour, I was quickly taken in by the well-ordered routine of suburban Melbourne where the profoundest conversation turned around the weather, television or football. Consuming goods and services was the ideal, and polite exchange of platitudes the peak of social activity. But the bliss of ever-flowing ice-cold beer provided a change from the hot and garbage-littered streets of Tel-Aviv.

71

I had not sought the assignment, but rather it had fallen into my hands as if by fate – a prophecy come true – but I was mistaken. I became aware of my error on one of the numerous occasions in which the United Nations Security Council voted to brand Israel the aggressor. An Australian businessman entered my office and, brandishing a newspaper, pointed triumphantly to the headline:

'You see, David, again you are the aggressors.'

'Since we crucified Jesus,' I replied, 'we are always the aggressors.'

That ended our friendship, my mission and my intended settlement in Australia. I returned to the Israel Ghetto-State, exchanging personal for collective insecurity.

Little did I know how close to the truth my 1943 prediction would come in later years. Having been wrong about Australia, I was almost right about the Jewish State. There was a systematic suppression of the truth concerning the role played by the Jewish leadership in Palestine and in the United States, in the ghettos and in the concentration camps, along with the acceptance of German 'reparations'. It was followed by a total disregard of traditional Jewish values and moral concepts. The army, victorious on the battlefield, became the idol of the nation, the screen behind which corruption, drugs and other evils were to be hidden.

At one incident army and police became as effective as the Jewish police in the Kovno Ghetto. There, a Jew could be killed with impunity by any German or Lithuanian guard or drunk. In the Jewish State of Israel, any Arab who kills a Jew – 'acting from nationalistic motives' (as the news media repeat without comment and thereby condone and legitimize the killings) – can count on full protection from the police, the army and the courts, and, considering that they are often being released before serving their terms as 'gestures' of appeasement, or in exchange for hostages, literally get away with murder. The two young murderers of the women whose 'only crime was being Jewish' were to be sentenced to nineteen years' imprisonment.[21]

Then the Jewish authorities had to please their German masters. Now, they do their best to please their American benefactors.

THE CHILDREN

The news that the Germans had started to incinerate the bodies of the people they had killed at the Ninth Fort was being interpreted as a 'good sign'. Since they were trying to hide the traces of their mass shootings from the advancing Russians, it seemed obvious that they did not intend to create new proof of their activities. But these wishful theories soon gave way to rumours that the Germans were now taking all Jews to Poland where they were killing them by gas and burning them in huge furnaces. These rumours became the subject of my conversations with Yoheved as we returned home from work. We tried to imagine how the Germans were doing it, but mostly we talked about how to escape from the Ghetto. There was no doubt in our minds that in the end they would kill us all. Only my father, having been asked what he thought about the gas, dismissed my mother's misgivings as nonsense.

People started to build underground shelters. During the night, earth was moved from one place to another. Yoheved told me that in her house lived a very rich man who was stocking food in his 'bunker'. He intended to hide there with his wife from the moment the Germans started anything until the Russians came. One could obtain the privilege of hiding by helping out with digging or other work needed for the construction of the bunkers. I offered my services through Yoheved, but they did not trust me; not because of me, but because of my father. I understood.

I brooded day and night about a way to escape. I said nothing anymore to anybody. The rumours that many people were leaving the Ghetto to join the partisans increased my despair; because whenever I made the most guarded allusion to the subject, people would laugh in my face. Yoheved thought that it might be because I was too young. Then, she herself left the Ghetto without telling me anything. Her parents had found her a hiding place with a peasant family in a village not far away. A week after her absence from work, her best friend Miriam came to tell me that Yoheved hoped to see me again after the war. She handed me a small enamelled pendant with a picture of Moses on one side and the Ten Commandments on the other. Yoheved's message to me was that if I kept them, she was sure that we would meet again after the war. I made a miniature metal box for it which I always carried in my pocket.

The Russian advances on the Dnieper and the Dniester, coupled with rumours about a second front that the Americans and the British were soon going to open in western Europe, encouraged those who believed that everything was now 'practically over'. Combined with the early spring, these rumours created an atmosphere of optimism, especially amongst the young. It was shattered by a black passenger car with a loudspeaker on the roof:

'Achtung, Achtung! Wer auf die Strasse geht wird sofort erschossen (Attention, Attention! Whoever goes outside will be shot immediately),' repeating the warning as it continued its way through the streets of the Ghetto. A truck arrived behind the fence at the end of the field stretching out from the workshops. Fully-armed soldiers jumped down and took up positions every ten yards. The Ghetto was being surrounded.

There was complete silence in the workshop. No sound came from the first floor from where the noise of sewing machines usually reverberated through the ceiling. Everybody was staring through the windows above their workbenches. At the same time, Jewish Ghetto policemen assembled and formed three ranks just outside the workshop. High-ranking officers inspected boots and brassards. Two army trucks arrived; four Germans got out, ordered the policemen into the trucks and drove off.

Nobody said a word; nobody touched a tool; everyone was paralyzed. The chief instructor came into the workshop and ordered everyone back to work. If any Germans came, they should find us all at work. He was sure that nothing would happen to us, as long as we were working.

The clanging of tools had started again when the door was kicked open by two Germans with their guns drawn. They asked how old everyone was. Everyone said sixteen, except for one boy of small build who said fifteen as he hammered away at a piece of metal. The Germans left. It was not until late in the afternoon that someone remembered to put the kettle on. We stayed well after closing time sipping the hot water, because we were too scared to go out into the street.

When darkness fell, the loudspeaker car went by again:

'Achtung, Achtung! Die Uebung ist vorueber. Alle

duerfen auf die Strasse! (Attention, attention! The exercise is over. Everyone is allowed on the street!)'

We cleaned up and went home. As I reached the main street which ran from the river past the Aeltestenrat to the Ghetto gate, I heard screams around me coming from every window.

'Yossele, where are you?' 'Sorele . . .'

The voices came from all around. A woman was standing at a first-floor window pulling her hair out and screaming. As I was staring at the woman and thinking that maybe she had gone mad, a passerby told me that they had taken away all the children.

As I continued on my way, the thought entered my mind that maybe they had taken my brother too; but no sooner had I opened the door than my mother pointed to the ceiling and whispered that Hans was beneath the roof. If she had told me that the Germans had taken him away, I would have felt the same – nothing at all.

I wanted the bread ration, but the lottery could only be started after my father came back from work. When he returned, the bread was allotted in the absence of my brother. This time, my mother had the upper hand. Against her husband's wishes to bring the 'small one' down, she had insisted that he stay hidden for at least one more day. After everyone was in bed, she reached up to the ceiling by climbing on a chair placed on the table, and handed Hans the bread, some water, and an apple. I didn't see the apple in the darkness, but I recognized its smell. I wondered where she had found it.

The next morning, March 28, 1944, everybody went to work as usual. I saw the chief instructor sitting in his office, staring out of the window. He did not return my greeting nor did he turn his head. His two girls had been taken away. Some of the seamstresses were crying as they went up the stairs, and everybody was idling around. Someone said that the policemen had all been taken to the Ninth Fort. At first nobody wanted to believe it; but then we realized that they were gone, as everyone recalled not having seen them since the day before when they had been driven off. We could not guess why they had been taken there.

All of a sudden, the door was kicked open and the soldiers shouted: 'Alles raus! (Everyone out!)'

Once outside, we were led to the toolshed where everyone was given a pickaxe and a shovel. The two Germans took us to the square adjoining the Ghettokommandantur (office of the German Ghetto commander) near the gate. There they left us under the care of our chief instructor who assigned two men each to dig holes for fence posts. The ground was hard and work proceeded slowly.

The Ghetto gate was opened wide. Three army trucks drove in and lined up in a row with their back-ends towards us. Six Germans, three of them with wolfhounds, descended from the trucks and started playing with the dogs. The trucks were followed by several motorcycles, each manned by two Germans and a Jewish policeman in the sidecar. ('After having been tortured and having witnessed the execution of their commanding officers at the Ninth Fort, about ninety Jewish policemen were released and returned to the Ghetto. Of course, among the released were also all those who gave in under torture and agreed to disclose the bunkers in the Ghetto.'[22]) The motorcycles turned off into the Ghetto.

The holes were not yet completed when the first group of children arrived in the square. Those who were sufficiently grown up climbed on the first truck. The smaller ones were grabbed and thrown in after them. Their cries increased at the sight of the dogs barking at them when they were already on the trucks. Some came under German guard; some were brought by Jewish policemen. The smaller ones came with their mothers. The dogs jumped at the mothers, separating them from their children. Some women tried to get into the truck with their infants, but the dogs were trained to jump at their throats making them release their hold. Children who fell were grabbed by their limbs and thrown onto the truck. As soon as it was full, it drove off.

The shrieks of those little children being driven away follow me throughout the years, causing me to tremble whenever I see a crying child. Fifteen years later, one of my daughters, who was then six years old, was bitten by her pet and started to cry. I tried to strangle the little dog, as the whole scene of dogs biting children appeared again before my eyes.

However, then, as I stood there with my pickaxe, I only thought about how fortunate I was to be sixteen already, to be 'useful', knowing that nothing would happen to me. I finished digging my hole and moved on to the next one. The fence had to be completed by nightfall.

The children's Aktion had a numbing effect. Those children who had not been dragged out of their hiding places, like my brother, were not allowed onto the street during the day. Russian victories were a poor consolation for parents robbed of their children whose fate had become general knowledge. The name of Auschwitz, the gas chambers and crematoria, dominated every conversation still with the qualification that only the old and the very young were being gassed. The myth of Germans needing Jewish craftsmen was still current, but mostly being used to alleviate despair.

The former vocational training centre was closed down, and I was assigned to an army workshop at Kovno airport where Russian heavy guns were being adapted to German-calibre shells. I developed very friendly relations with the German in charge of the workshop. Nevertheless, getting up at five and being marched for one hour from the Ghetto to the airport on an empty stomach created a feeling of raging despair, which I could overcome only by contemplating escape. The German was so satisfied with my diligence and the precision of my work that every day he brought me a sausage sandwich, and we sat and ate together under a giant jacked-up gun barrel. He spoke to me about Gelsenkirchen, his home town. I told him about Austria. Once he suggested that maybe he would be able to get me a German uniform and take me home with him as soon as 'we' were able to go back. He felt that the war was lost, and with the Unordnung (disorder) everywhere, he was sure we could get through. Then, when the war was over, we could open up a workshop together. I already saw myself riding on a train, wearing a German uniform complete with belt and boots, going to Germany, eating sausage sandwiches.

One day he disappeared. The sergeant who replaced him ate his breakfast by himself, while I continued operating the lathe.

Another way of escape had to be found. 'From December 1943 till March 24, 1944, about 280 people, including about eighty women, were taken from the Ghetto. Most of them were absorbed in the partisan division "Death to the Conquerors".'[23] Not being able to make any contact with the people in the Ghetto who were organizing groups to join the partisans, I decided to get there on my own. I knew that they were located about seven miles down the river which flowed past the Ghetto. There, the woods almost reached the river; and if I could swim downstream, I might reach them undetected. Jews were permitted to bath in the river, so I thought that by staying under the water long enough, I would be carried downstream for at least half a mile: and the German guards would assume that I had drowned.

As I was sitting at the dinner table and calculating distances on the map of Lithuania, my father suddenly appeared. He asked me what I was doing; and when I answered that I wasn't doing anything, he slapped me, took hold of my arm and dragged me outside. I tried to pull myself loose, but he was much stronger than I. He continued dragging me behind him and calling me a dirty dog who ought to be shot. I realized that he wanted to take me to the Kommandantur. I started screaming for him to let me go, but I was afraid to hit him or kick him, because I still had not forgotten the Torah lesson that whoever raises a hand against his father or his mother is to be stoned to death. That by disappearing from the Ghetto I would condemn them and my brother to certain death, did not fall under the same prohibition. I only remembered Mr Kurz telling me about 'a hand raised in rebellion' (Deuteronomy 21:18). However, running away before they would kill us all was not 'rebellion'.

While I was struggling and shouting, a woman stepped out from one of the houses and blocked our way. She obviously knew my father. In an authoritative manner, she inquired what he was doing.

'I am taking him straight to the Gestapo. He plans to escape, and I don't intend to be shot because of this dirty dog here.'

I had recognized the woman as Masha, of whom it was rumoured that she was connected with the communists who were the only ones capable of getting people to the partisans. I admitted my intentions when she asked me whether my father was telling the truth. She listened to my story of how I wanted to escape on my own because I had no connections, and then she invited us into her room for a talk.

She asked us to sit down and offered us hot water. She told us that if I would promise not to try to escape on my own, she would see to it that someone she knew would take the four of us 'to the woods'. They needed doctors there. There was fighting every day, and the wounded lacked sufficient medical attention.

'Kommt nicht in Frage (Out of the question),' he said in the clipped German he had adopted and rose to leave.

'Up to you Doctor; but if you hand your son over to the Germans, your life might also be in danger.'

'What do you mean?!'

'Just think it over, Doctor. Let your son go. He won't escape.'

I took that as an implied promise that she might help me get to the partisans with a group. A few days later, she came to our house to ask me to repair the lock on her door. When I refused to accept payment, she told me that bribes would not get me what I wanted. When I asked what would get me there, she answered that one day I would find out by myself.

That day never came.

BETRAYAL

On July 3, 1944, the Russians recaptured Minsk and were advancing towards Vilna, situated only about eighty miles away from Kovno. Whilst earlier, any news of Russian victories or advances had given rise to new hope, this time near hysteria broke out. People stopped going to work. From hour to hour, the fear of deportation rose. Evacuation was imminent.

Yet for many, life continued as usual. Summer always brought out strollers who walked up and down Varniu Street – the main street leading to the Ghetto gate – enjoying the sunset, in hopeful chatter about the expected early end of the war; they were mostly youngsters and their girls, flirting, joking as they had done before the war on Liberty Avenue.

Others tried desperately to escape. A group of eleven young men between the ages of eighteen and twenty-two decided to break through a barred wooden gate at the end of the street running past an old Christian cemetery. The escape had been planned for the early morning; but the night before, one of them – intimidated by the German threat that relatives of escapees would be shot – informed the Jewish police who, in turn, denounced them to the Germans. When the group rushed the gate, they were cut down by machine guns hidden in the growth of the cemetery. The ten bodies were laid out in a row on Varniu Street as a warning. All had been shot in the head; dried blood was on cheeks and foreheads, flies crawling over faces into open mouths forming clusters around the eyes.

Yet, the young people of the Ghetto continued strolling past as if the ten dead Jews were simply part of the reddish ground on which they lay – their eyes wide open staring into the sky in horror. Nobody stopped. Nobody looked. Nobody said Kaddish (prayer for the dead) for the minyan (minimum ten men required for group prayer) laid out in a row, silently accusing with contorted features those who had given them away and those who did not care.

I met the dead again on July 6, 1989, when sixteen Jews were killed by an Arab who had diverted a bus into a ravine. Of course, there were the curious who, thirsting for sensation, stopped their cars at the spot where the disaster had occurred on the road from Tel-Aviv to Jerusalem. They watched the corpses being pulled up from the ravine, as if it were just another horror movie on television. There were those who helped to remove the survivors and the bodies of the dead. There were others who found no outlet for their rage. But the leaders and the media – in their routine of protecting the precarious balance of Jewish-Arab relations – continued blaring pronouncements and commentaries while murdered Jews were being dragged from the ravine, their 'only' sin having been 'being Jewish' as established by the judges from Beersheva.

I only saw the ten, lined up dead on the Kovno Ghetto promenade, betrayed by their own.

EVACUATION

The evacuation order was announced a few days later. Food supplies were stopped; the Ghetto was sealed; work was discontinued. No one was allowed in or out. While many sought refuge in hurriedly constructed hideouts where they intended to await the advancing Russians, there were those who, like my father, wanted to be the first to be evacuated. Those arriving first at the assembly square were promised preferential transport facilities. They were to travel by boat to Germany.

There was no doubt that with the end of the war and the German defeat in sight, no more Jews would be killed. They needed every man to stop the Russians from overrunning Europe. And they could not afford to be branded by the world as murderers. Even they had admitted it.

My father had spoken to the Ghettokommandant himself, who had promised to personally supervize the safe arrival of all the inmates of the KZ-Kauen (as the Kovno Ghetto was renamed in 1943), by accompanying them to Germany.

Everybody was allowed to take ten kilos. On the morning of July 8, 1944, we set out to the assembly square, wearing our best clothes, each of us carrying a small bundle with extra shirts, some underwear and shoes. My mother kept the food – a loaf of bread, some butter, a thermos with hot water. My father carried his instrument case in the event that first aid was needed on the Reise (the German equivalent of the English 'journey' but also conveying a mood of anticipated joy). In that mood, despite having left behind all our possessions – toys and tools, pictures and mementos, all of real and sentimental value – we followed my father cheerfully in the morning sun to the square where we were received by SS guards. They ordered us to sit down in rows of five so we could be counted.

We sat down on our bundles, while my father went to have a word with one of the SS officers. When he returned, he told us and the people sitting near us that as soon as 600 people were assembled, we would be taken to the 'ship'.

There we would be issued food rations. With that prospect, my mother divided the loaf of bread and we emptied the thermos. She discarded it, because she said we wouldn't need it anymore. The butter had melted in the heat. More people were still arriving in the square; some on their own, others accompanied by Jewish policemen.

Shortly before sunset, we were marched through the gate. Lithuanians watched from their windows as we slowly went past, guarded by not more than six or eight German soldiers. Marching order was not strictly observed, and the column proceeded at a leisurely pace.

All of a sudden, my mother took a few steps forward, overtaking three ranks marching in front of us, crossed the sidewalk and disappeared in an open doorway. When we reached it a few seconds later, she beckoned to us to join her. Dusk had fallen, and it could be done without attracting the attention of the guards who followed the column from behind.

'Come back here immediately!' my father barked.

Fearing to be caught, she returned to the ranks and took my brother's hand, continuing to march silently until we reached the river. By then it was completely dark. Again we had to sit and wait for embarkation at dawn; no lights were allowed. Permission was given to relieve ourselves at the wall enforcing the slope rising from the quay. The approach road leading into the town was deserted. I only had to tear off the yellow stars and walk away. Nobody would have noticed, except my father; and he would immediately have notified the Transportfuehrer (Convoy leader).

I returned to my place, and sharing a bundle with my brother, I tried to get some sleep on the concrete ground which still held some warmth from the heat of the summer day.

Up the river towards Vilna, flares lit up the sky and the rumble of distant artillery fire could be heard. The sun was rising when we awoke. Two barges linked to a tug were lined up at the quay, and within an hour all six hundred people had crossed the boarding planks down into the holds of the two boats. Every person had been handed a package of army biscuits and a package of margarine for four. Two men were carrying aboard huge canisters of drinking water. The barges' bows and sterns had been partitioned off, with four German guards per barge quartered behind the partitions. A machine-gun was placed on the stern of the first barge. Right beneath it on the bottom of the hold, six feet down, we settled next to the partition.

We tried to find the most comfortable position in the overcrowded hold, but there was only space to stretch or sit on a bundle. Nobody could move without stepping on someone else. There were no portholes, and all we could see was the sky above the open hold.

The engine started thumping; the waves of the river splashed against the planks; a slight swaying movement caused some people to vomit. We were on our way to Germany.

Next morning, they distributed more biscuits, margarine and marmalade. Then, the men were allowed one by one up the narrow deck to relieve themselves into the river. Buckets were provided for the women, who shielded each other while attending to their needs. As I climbed up the ladder, I saw that the machine gun had been left unattended while the guards were playing cards behind the partition below. Looking down into the hold, I tried to make out

RIVER CONVOY

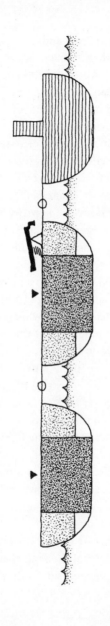

1 〰〰〰 — Water line

2 ▦▦▦ — Tug

3 ▶ — Barges

4 ░░░ — Partitioned Areas

5 ▓▓▓ — Holds

6  — Abandoned Machinegun

someone who had been in the army and might know how to operate the weapon. My father probably knew, having been a soldier in the First World War, but I did not trust him.

I found a possible candidate and worked my way through by stepping over crouching people – some of them stretching out their legs, most of them grumbling at my disturbing them. My guess was right. The man had served in the Lithuanian army, but my entreaties were in vain. All he had to do was direct the gun into the partitioned hold and shoot, but he refused to do it. There was no need for it. We were all going to be working in Germany, as my father had assured his fellow passengers over and over again. He had become some sort of Transportoberjude, handing out headache pills.

As the journey continued, four or five people at a time were allowed on deck to admire the peaceful landscape, its pastoral serenity and the woods in which the partisans were hiding. I considered jumping into the river to swim the relatively short distance to the woods, but I dismissed the idea. I might be shot while in the water.

On the third day out at sea, we were informed through my father that we were going to Koenigsberg. The very name of the centuries-old German town raised hopes; but the desolate view of the sandy banks of the Baltic Sea, which stretched to an almost horizonless end, gave the sound of Koenigsberg an unrealistic ring. The still unguarded machine gun and the voices of the guards celebrating the return to the Heimat with song and drink were reminders that hope was based on vain illusions.

As I stood on the deck, I remembered the metal box with Yoheved's Ten Commandments. Fearing that I would be searched on arrival, I took the pendant from its tiny locket, put it in my pocket, and with a last look at Yoheved's interlaced initials I had engraved on the locket cover, I dropped it into the sea. If they searched me. I would hide the pendant under my tongue.

We docked in Koenigsberg, but nobody was to leave the boats. Groups of two or three people were allowed on deck. I was surprised at the elegant look of the houses and the shiny streetcars, their bells clanging as if there were no war. A few well-dressed Jews, wearing yellow stars with the word 'Jude' printed on them in black script resembling Hebrew letters, came to visit us. Did they know when we would be let off the boat? Did they know where we were going? Questions were exchanged across the few inches of water separating the barges from the quay, but nobody had answers. At nightfall, the German Jews went home and we went back below. That Jews were free to walk the streets of Koenigsberg was interpreted as further proof that the Germans would keep their promise. Perhaps they were preparing suitable accommodations.

However, when we woke up the next morning and climbed up to the deck, we saw that we had put to sea again, skirting the coast on our left. We were on our way to Danzig. The Transportfuehrer had come especially to inform my father that there had been a change of plans. One more day and we would arrive. More biscuits, margarine and marmalade were handed out to keep us happy. For another night I listened to the water lapping against the hull – then we docked again.

Everything was grey. The sky, the sea, the sand stretching out behind the wharf – even the nearby forest with its trees neatly planted at equal intervals seemed to be covered with the grey dust from which they were growing.

'Los! Alles raus! (Go! Everybody out!)'

All of a sudden, dogs started barking. About twenty Germans surrounded us as we left the barges, some of them with dogs eager to attack.

'Los! Antreten! Schnell! (Go! Form ranks! Fast!)'

My father walked up to the Transportfuehrer.

'Hau ab! Du Schweinehund!' the German shouted.

A kick in his behind sent my father reeling to the ground. His instruments landed in the sand. Slowly he got up while a shove with a rifle butt brought him back into the ranks.

Schweinehund. I liked the double-barrelled insult. There is no equivalent invective in the English language fusing a pig and a dog into one word. I adopted the expression to the extent that even now I sometimes use it under my breath when I get angry.

My mother stared in front of her. My brother, the 'Bar Mitzvah bocher' as I used to call him contemptuously, was crying. I had had enough. To hell with them. No more father. No more mother. I felt that they were to blame for all our misfortunes – not so much my mother as my father. The Schweinehund. He had called me 'dirty dog'. Now I was free to do as I pleased.

I moved up front where there were not too many guards. The last ranks received most of the beatings. We marched through the woods, grey dust rising from the narrow road. I recalled all the times I could have escaped, but it was too late. Danzig? Where were we? An hour later, we came out of the woods.

CONCENTRATION CAMP

The most important experience of a concentration camp survivor is described by Primo Levi:

> I must repeat: we, the survivors, are not the true witnesses. This is an uncomfortable notion of which I have become conscious little by little, reading the memoirs of others and reading mine at a distance of years. We survivors are not only an exiguous but also an anomalous minority: we are those who by their prevarications or abilities or good luck did not touch bottom. Those who did so, those who saw the Gorgon, have not returned to tell about it, or have turned mute, but they are the 'Muslims', the submerged, the complete witnesses, the ones whose deposition would have a general significance. They are the rule, we are the exception.
>
> *The Drowned and the Saved*[24]

When I read these words, I concluded that there was nothing more to say. Yet, in the light of the continuing 'prevarications', especially from those who have turned their survival into a justification for their actions, and their recollections into a means of disguising the lies, I cannot continue my narrative without having quoted from that great spirit, the caution that we, the survivors, are not the 'true witnesses'.

Therefore, in weighing my decision whether to attempt to add anything to Primo Levi's observations, I found that there was one aspect of the wanton destruction of human beings by their fellow men that has not yet been sufficiently explored – the role of those who strove to turn from victim to perpetrator and who often succeeded.

A confession of such a survivor may perhaps contribute to the search for an interpretation of the immemorial riddle of human inhumanity – but it will not serve as justification.

STUTTHOF BEI DANZIG

Electrified barbed wire fences enclosed green army barracks with geraniums on the windowsills. Watch-towers every fifty yards. The gate slid open. We passed neatly-tended patches of grass in front of what appeared to be empty barracks and arrived at a huge shed with only one small iron door. They drove us through it with shouts and blows, and we found ourselves locked inside; clouds of dust rose from the concrete floor penetrating our mouths and nostrils. 'Gas!' I thought at first, but the grey dust settled on the ground again.

In the corner piled up in separate heaps were jackets, trousers, shoes. Like everybody else, I moved away from the narrow door which had been bolted on the outside and lay down, resting my head on my bundle. I was still trembling inside because of the scare of gas, but then I fell asleep in spite of continuous thoughts about bread and sausages which had been keeping me awake. I had never realized that being very hungry could become physically painful and that there was nothing else that mattered when one was craving for food.

In the morning, the door was opened and we were commanded to file out through the narrow opening. Outside, we were met by an SS officer who, with a riding whip, directed women and children to the right, men to the left. My mother pushed my brother to the left; but in spite of being quite tall, he clung to her, not letting go of her hand. He was taken away with the women and the few children who had escaped the Aktion in the Ghetto.

We were ordered to leave our bundles and to line up in front of a barrack marked Entlausung. We entered one by one, undressed totally, went under a shower, and still wet, lined up on a bench while men in striped prison clothes shaved our armpits, the intimate areas and finally, after we stepped down again, our heads. Each one was issued a cap, a pair of trousers, a jacket with a number sewn on the left sleeve – all striped grey and blue – a pair of wooden clogs, a plate and a spoon. After collecting our belts from the clothes left at the entrance, we went outside.

During the whole procedure, I had kept the pendant under my tongue; and I was proud of not having been caught when they checked our mouths for gold dentures. Having nearly swallowed it, I put the pendant in my pocket. My father looked funny without his hair and without the golden glint of the denture which had replaced the teeth the Christian god had knocked out with his feet.

Bread. Bread. The word went round and round in my mind, my stomach, before my eyes. I tried to push air into my stomach the way we did at school to emit a burp. I started scanning the ground. Maybe someone had left some bread in one of the bundles which were still where we had left them.

The sudden command to line up prevented me from

93

continuing my search. We lined up in five ranks and were drilled: 'Muetzen ab! Muetzen auf! (Caps off! Caps on!)'

We were commanded to slap our caps on the upper thigh to produce a clapping sound. After half an hour's exercise, we were marched off to our quarters, coming to a halt between two barracks: 'In die Baracken! (Into the barracks!)'

Everyone hesitated, not knowing which way to turn. Suddenly, out of nowhere, appeared strong and well-fed prisoners wearing black arm bands with the word Kapo (supervisor) written on it. They started chasing us with rubber truncheons. I chose the nearest door and climbed into one of the upper bunks where it would be harder for them to reach me. My father got in below.

We were no sooner settled when a command brought us out again. This time, the Kapos waited on both sides of the door and hit everyone with their truncheons as we came out. I pushed behind my father and ducked at the right moment. He was hit twice, while I escaped without a blow.

'Caps down! Caps up!' The whole thing started over again, until shortly before nightfall, when two men were taken by one of the Kapos to bring the soup. They returned carrying a steaming canister followed by the Kapo with a ladle. A slice of bread was handed out with the soup. I had finished while others were still lining up, so I lined up again.

'Dankeschoen Herr Blockaeltester,' I said as I read what was written on his armband. Noticing my German, he asked where I was from. When I told him that I was from Innsbruck, he said that he was also from there; and he handed me another slice of bread. I asked him what the green triangle beneath his number meant, and he told me

94

that it was the sign for 'criminal'. The red triangles meant 'political'. He had been sent to Stutthof because he had killed his parents with an axe.

When I returned to our quarters, my father asked me to bring him some more soup too; but I told him to fetch it himself.

As I lay on my bunk, I wanted to have a look at Yoheved's pendant before I went to sleep, but I could not find it. Panicking, I turned my pockets inside out. It wasn't there. I had lost the 'Ten Commandments'.

It became the daily start of camp routine to line up outside the barrack for hours, to be counted over and over again, after having been driven with rubber truncheons from washroom through latrine for hurried perfunctory ablutions and a short sojourn on an open row of toilets – fear preventing us from performing. This was followed by the distribution of coffee – a black-brown liquid, bitter but providing an illusionary filling of the stomach.

For the rest of the day, we were marched up and down the electrical fence, drilled in 'caps down-caps up', jumping with our knees bent and holding out our hands in front, stumbling over one another as the weaker ones fell down, brought up again by blows from ox-tail whips which the Kapos wielded during 'exercises'. I always managed to be up front, to jump and run as soon as I heard the commands, to avoid the blows, taking care not to stumble. Whoever did was either trampled by those who followed or hit while getting up.

How did one become a Kapo? Or a Blockaeltester? They had better uniforms. They were always neat and clean. They obviously enjoyed what they were doing, yet they were also prisoners. Whenever a German appeared, they too brought down their caps on their thighs, standing at attention until the German had passed. If I became an 'officer', as I designated the bearers of the black arm bands, I might be permitted to beat even my father now that there was really no more 'Superior Policeman' as he had said. One could do anything without fear of what was written in the Torah.

THE WOMEN

At first, the women on the other side of the fence did not look like women at all. We knew they were, because they were in the Frauenlager (women's camp). With their heads shaven, they looked like men in skirts. The sounds reaching us were as if there was continuous fighting going on, but then we realized that the women were being chased around and beaten too. Their shrieks continued throughout the day.

When my mother called out my name, I did not recognize her at first. When she threw a slice of bread across the fence, I remembered her features. The bread landed a few feet in front of me; and before anybody could beat me to it, I grabbed and stuffed a big chunk into my mouth.

'Share it with father!' she called, but I had already swallowed all of it.

The following day, she threw it to my father who lost it fighting off the others. Other women threw bread over the fence. I wondered why. I would not have done it. Maybe they were given more than they could eat.

My father asked me if I had seen my brother.

'No!'

To me he was dead already.

TRANSFER

The attempt on Hitler's life on July 20, 1944 affected the daily routine at Stutthof only slightly. Exercises lasted less time than usual. Kapos huddled in groups, but we heard only rumours. Nobody knew whether he was dead, but even if he was, the Kapos and the guards on the turrets – machine-guns ready to shoot anybody approaching the fence – were still alive.

In the evening, Heini, my friend from Innsbruck, whispered to me while he ladled soup onto my plate that Hitler was still alive and that they would be moving us down to Dachau in the morning. He advised me to show my muscles during medical inspection and wished me good luck.

'What did he tell you?' my father asked.

'Nothing.'

A few days later, we were put on a freight train after having been examined by an SS doctor, who squeezed everyone's balled muscles of the right arm and decided who was to be sent back to the barracks or to leave for Dachau.

'Ich bin Arzt, Herr Doktor (I am a physician, Herr Doctor),' my father said while holding out his arm.

'Halt die Fresse und hau ab! (Shut your trap and get lost).' The German slapped him across the face and pushed him into the ranks of those destined to travel.

I managed to get away from him at the ramp where we

were loaded into box cars. Fifty men with two guards to a box car. Crossing what was formerly Poland, we went past stations bearing names I still remembered from my trip north, when we had travelled from Austria to Lithuania. Six years had passed since then.

They allowed us to get some water at small deserted railway stations as we continued through the night, arriving in the afternoon of the second day at a small place called Utting, a village in central Bavaria. This was one of ten locations near which forced labour camps were situated around Landsberg am Lech, Kreis Kaufering, and which were administered under the jurisdiction of the Dachau Concentration Camp. Three hundred men were counted off, and the rest were chased back into the train – my father among them.

After being led to a small wood, we walked through it as if on an excursion. Some picked up mushrooms, only to discard them for fear of poisoning. I picked a few berries. We broke ranks while mounting the narrow path winding up between the trees to the top of a hill, but we were quickly reassembled in ranks of five in order to listen to a speech.

It seemed unusual that the speaker was an Oberfeldwebel (Sergeant Major) of the Wehrmacht (Regular army). The guards were from the SS, not more than ten surrounding the glade which had been cleared from growth and trees. Would they shoot us? There was only one barrack. There was no kitchen and no Entlausung. Nothing. Only one shed like the ones used on construction sites for tools and shelter.

After the usual 'caps down-caps up', the Oberfeldwebel informed us that we had come to Germany to work; that everybody who did his job properly would get enough food; that malingerers would be severely punished. Work was to start immediately or else we would have to sleep out in the open. Barracks and fence had to be completed by nightfall.

Foremen were chosen, each of them taking a detail of ten men. Shovels and pickaxes were issued. Fenceposts, barbed wire, boards and cement had all been prepared. Having been assigned to a group carrying boards, I realized that by placing myself in the middle, I could rest while the load was shared by the one preceding and the other following me. When they discovered my trick, they decided to take turns.

A ditch five feet deep, six feet wide and twelve yards long formed the bottom of the hut over which a roof was constructed. Standing in the middle of the ditch, we could almost touch the gabled roof which sloped down from its peak to the ground. The ground was covered with boards from the end of the roof to the ditch. We could sit down with our feet dangling in the ditch or lie down, head in the corner formed by roof and ground.

All the huts were completed late at night by moonlight. We settled down, twenty-five men on one side, twenty-five on the other, facing each other across the ditch. The following day, we covered the roofs with patches of turf, closed one end of the huts with a window and the other with a door. A foot and a half-wide lying space per person obliged us not to bend our legs and all to choose identical positions.

An underground airfield was to be built near the camp. Every morning we marched out, guarded by SS and led by the foremen who had become Kapos, after having been distinguished with the appropriate black arm bands.

GROUND HUT

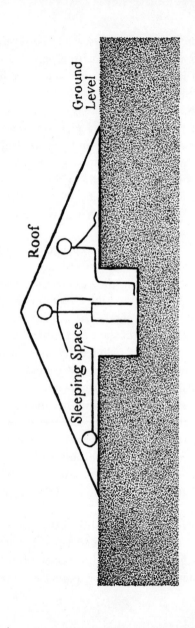

I quickly realized that my constant pushing away from my father had landed me in a group of people from the Shavli Ghetto in northern Lithuania where I didn't know a soul. Former Ghetto policemen and Judenrat officials had offered their experienced services immediately upon leaving the train. They all got the lighter jobs, while I, whose former status as Dr Haber's son was totally useless, was assigned to digging or carrying sacks of cement on my back.

This had to change. I was a locksmith. I spoke German. Maybe I could speak to one of the men in the Organisation Todt (paramilitary construction and engineering corps whose members supervized slave labourers). But I was hungry. I constantly searched the ground near the toolshed where the OT men met at lunchtime and where I had once found some potato peels. I could not run. Several times, I collapsed under a load of cement.

As winter approached, I made myself a shirt from a discarded cement bag. It protected at least the upper part of my body from the lice that had settled in all the seams of my jacket, which like all the others, I wore tucked into my trousers where lice crawled around between my legs. But most of them lived under the collar. We spent hours squeezing them between the fingernails of our thumbs, but for every one we caught there seemed to be two the next evening.

I could not leave the site to try and have a word with one of the Germans, because the Kapo watched us all the time. He even used to go after anybody who stayed in the latrine for more than five minutes, chasing them back to work – some of them with their pants still down.

As I grew hungrier every day, a sense of despair began to affect my behaviour. My eyes were constantly directed to the ground, hoping to find something edible. I shuffled about in my wooden clogs, exposing myself to blows because of my slow progress when marching to work or when carrying boards or cement. I started crying for no reason at all – tears would flow without my being able to stop them.

Every morning at the same time, a passenger train passed by the site. Once somebody killed himself by rushing up the embankment exactly as the train passed. I hadn't seen it, but the people talked about it in the barrack. They said that he was crazy for killing himself now that the war was almost over. I didn't think so.

My hut neighbour, a frail youngster of about fifteen, prayed from the moment he finished his ration of bread and coffee until he fell asleep. He too was crying, but that was natural. He was already a Muselmann (the German nickname for emaciated, almost totally fleshless human beings in their last stages of life, derived from Dervish, i.e. Muslim friars vowed to austerity). He was so skinny that he was a certain candidate to go to heaven via the chimney or otherwise. What I had not realized was that I too had become a Muselmann, only instead of praying, I constantly thought of how it would feel when I put my neck on the rail. Whether my skin would freeze onto the metal in the frost. In a way, I felt as I had in the Ghetto when I was planning to escape.

I started to calculate the exact arrival of the train from the time I heard its whistle. Every day, I put if off; but finally one day when I was feeling desperately cold and hopeless, I dropped my shovel and ran across the site, stumbling and getting up again, until I reached the rails. I had arrived too early. Two men rushed up after me and dragged me straight to the foreman's shed. They told him that I had tried to kill myself. The Chief Engineer, a German in civilian clothes, wanted to know why.

'Because I am hungry, Herr Baumeister,' I said, trying to hold back my tears.

Hearing my German, he inquired where I came from. I told him and added that I was a locksmith.

'Get the prisoner some bread and see that he gets work suited to his trade.'

The next morning my number was called up at roll-call, and I was transferred to the forge to become the smith's assistant. I was ridiculed for a few days by my hutmates, but I soon forgot the railway as I basked in the warmth of the fire. The smith was a Jew from Shavli and was always smoking cigarettes. I never found out how and from where he got them.

Even though I was warm, I was still hungry. It was part of the concentration camp system to distribute just enough food to keep the inmates working and obedient, preferring their slow demise to instant extermination. The 'Hungerbohrer' (hunger drill), as it was called by the higher concentration camp authorities, was a tool as much as the whip or the barbed wire. The Germans realized that total lack of food might cause even 'the hands of the pitiful women to cook their own children' (Lamentations, 4: 10); or, as rumour had it, in the Russian prisoner-of-war camps anyone who dropped dead was cut up, cooked and eaten – palms of the hands being the choice bit. The Germans also realized that hungry people do not revolt. Neither do they have the physical strength nor the mental stamina to take individual or organized action. They knew that if they wanted to rule efficiently, they had to let the inmates of any camp, prison or detention centre starve – but not completely – thus assuring obedience and, in many cases, even gratitude. Such as mine to the German engineer who ordered the Kapo to get me a slice of bread.

CHRISTMAS

My wife does not understand how, after all these years, I still do not like potatoes. Yet the explanation is very simple. I had eaten too many of them.

The Germans had a habit of stocking up on potatoes during autumn in preparation for the winter. In war and peace-time alike, they always filled their cellars with potatoes. To supply the many people working in the area, trainload after trainload of potatoes arrived at the very spot where I had tried to kill myself, to be unloaded by the prisoners of Arbeitslager Zehn (Labour Camp 10) as we were called.

The raw potatoes could be stolen, but the forge was the only place where they could be cooked. Because of the regular search at the gate, they could not be brought into the camp and consequently had to be consumed at the site. I made a kettle holding about two gallons of water out of aluminium which was cut off the abandoned fuselage of a downed American bomber, and the smith and I went into business.

Ten raw potatoes got you five cooked ones, and we split the booty fifty-fifty. On the first day, I ate six. The second day ten. The third day, ten in the morning and ten in the afternoon, putting another ten away for the next day. But

I had to spend the whole night and most of the next day in the latrine vomiting. I forgot the taste of the first potato, but I shall never forget the taste of the last. I keep being reminded of it whenever I see or smell potatoes.

Previously the lice would dance only at night in the warmth of the hut, which had been equipped with a stove for the winter. Now, they danced whenever I approached the open furnace in the smithy. I let the lice burst, instead of crushing them between my nails, by singeing them with a heated piece of iron. The smith threatened to denounce me. He didn't want me to be caught killing lice while I was supposed to be holding the steel pipes he was bending in the fire.

I was tormented by hunger again. The lice brought on a rage I could only still by scratching. To be seen scratching could result in being examined by the 'Lagerarzt' (camp physician) for typhus. He was Jewish and worked in the 'hospital', a barrack with four beds used in cases of work accidents. Nobody ever came out from there alive. Typhus examinations ended in transfer to Dachau – to the ovens.

I took to leaving the workshop in order to search for useable metal whenever the lice started dancing. Under this pretext, I approached the foremen's shed in the hope of finding offals, peels, anything, bringing the smith a piece of rail or some scraps of aluminium to keep him happy. He had started a small aluminium kettle business. I made the kettles, and he sold them to the Germans in exchange for cigarettes. He needed cigarettes more than bread. I got neither.

On my daily 'rounds', I noticed that one of the OT men hid his bag every morning between the girders of the crane serving the site. At noon, he would come back for it, take out bread, a sausage, and a bottle of beer and sit down under the crane to have his lunch.

White bread and a sausage!

This was the only time in my life that I felt what I later knew to be ambition. I had to get that bag no matter what. If they caught me, I reckoned it was better to die quickly with a full stomach than slowly, day after day, with that aching hole inside, below my ribs, which could never be filled. I kept observing the man when he arrived in the morning, hid his food and disappeared somewhere beyond the railway tracks which we were forbidden to cross. At midday, I watched him eating. Every day.

One morning, the whole area was covered with fog. My master allowed me to go to the latrine; but instead I went straight to the crane, reached up, grabbed the bag and hid under a shed built on pillars, two feet above the ground. I lay on my side, hidden by the grass and devoured the sausage, tearing a small corner from the white bread, stuffing it into my mouth until I had had enough. I abandoned the bag with what remained of the German's lunch and returned to the forge. It had taken only a few minutes.

A Christmas tree was erected in the middle of the Appellplatz (parade ground). Nobody knew what for. There was not a single Christian prisoner in Arbeitslager Zehn. But there were about three hundred Jews lined up that night, waiting for the one who had stolen the foreman's ration to step forward. 'All will suffer for one,' the Oberfeldwebel announced. As long as the man would not give himself up, everybody would stand at attention. And everybody stood – for hours through half the night.

It started snowing. A single light from the watch-tower illuminated the scene. Nobody suspected me, because nobody had seen me. Like everybody, I was freezing. An irrational yearning kept ruminating in my mind: to find protection from the cold by being able to hide within my own body where somewhere inside the belly it was still warm. Yet, it was seeing the Oberfeldwebel stomping his feet and the guards marching up and down in order to keep warm, which sustained my conviction that in the end they'd let us go.

I looked at the Christmas tree and suddenly remembered 'Silent Night, Holy Night . . .', the song my schoolmates were practising while I had to wait outside the classroom during Catechism class, memorizing the melody in spite of myself. That was the result of bread and sausage – 'sweet childhood memories'.

I froze, but for once the lice didn't dance. When I finally settled on the flattened straw, I experienced for the first time in my life what I learned to classify as happiness. I had had them all. The Germans and the Jews. The Kapos and the guards.

Two people died that night from 'exposure' (as the Germans recorded in such cases), after they had collapsed on the ground. But I had succeeded.

There was one boy who knew. He slept right next to me. He was praying all the time, silently, but the whispering got on my nerves.

'Shut up!' I shouted.

'You should be ashamed of yourself.'

'Ashamed?!'

'Sure. You took the German's bread.'

I was dumbfounded. He had put two and two together. A few days earlier during the night, while he had gone to relieve himself, I had stolen his margarine ration which he had hidden between a beam and the roof. He used to save the margarine for breakfast. He could not prove it, but it was true. He died a few days later from under-nourishment and pneumonia which he had caught that night we spent outside.

When 'Silent Night' blares from sound systems in department stores around the world, when millions of Americans slaughter turkeys, when Jews greet their Christian 'fellow men' with 'Merry Christmas' – even in the Jewish State where the army radio wishes a happy holiday to 'all those among us who celebrate the feast of nativity'[25] – I recall the memory within the memory. I recall the silent holy night of Christmas 1944 when two Jews died because I had stolen food, while the melody ran through my head, not yet realizing that it was the hymn of those whose hatred of the Jews was their creed, whose followers were killing Jews as they had always done – in the shadow of their Christmas trees.

VALUES

Nietzsche calls his work, *The Will to Power*, 'an attempt at the revaluation of all values'. I did not know at the time that there was a whole philosophy based on the 'revaluation of all values' in the quest for power, nor was I aware of any need for 'revaluation'. Maybe now, the time has come to try and re-evaluate the values which brought us into concentration camps and those which sustained us there.

I myself dropped the few values I had left after the abolition of the 'Superior Policeman' and after I had stolen the German's sausage and my hut-mate's only portion of margarine, because *nobody* would see me. If I do not steal today – even when I am sure that nobody would find out – it is because of the mental acrobatics it would take to justify the deed, having painfully recovered, with the help of others, some of my discarded values. However, the experience that theft brings survival and the occasional urge to steal – not for the value of the object nor its necessity but to relive that sense of superiority arising from the helplessness of the victim – will probably accompany me for the rest of my life, together with the two apples I always carry with me in case I should suddenly be attacked by hunger.

As I am writing these lines, I feel as if I am being hunted by a force within me over which I wield no power; to get it over with; to conclude the story which should have ended fifty years ago, lest I die before it is completed; but which continues like the march for miles and miles on which I now must take the reader. And as I then had to keep going, step by step, to keep alive, I now must slowly work myself through facts and gathered experiences illuminating those which perhaps might assist the blind to prevent their being led again by the selfish and the perfidious into destruction.

KADDISH

When they asked for thirty volunteers for Lager Eins (Labour Camp 1) near Landsberg, I immediately stepped forward. I had learned that many Jews from Kovno were being held there and was sure that old acquaintances or former patients of my father might help me into a better position. I might even become a Kapo. There were also rumours that there was more food in Lager Eins. We still did not grasp the fact that whenever the German wanted to move a group of Jews, they circulated rumours that there was more food at their intended destination.

The fact that the camp was twenty miles away did not strike me as an obstacle. Having reasserted myself after my successful sausage theft, I thought I would be able to cover the distance easily. The SS doctor who examined us before we set out thought so too. Being both a doctor and an SS officer endowed him with double authority.

I even 'enjoyed' the snowed-in landscape, imagining the people inside the picturesque Bavarian cottages, warm and comfortable, having buttered rolls for breakfast. The single guard who accompanied us did not bother me nor did the others who marched at my side, as they tried to guess how much longer we would have to march or whether they were really taking us to Lager Eins. As we passed another village, I suddenly felt an enormous need to sit down – just for a few minutes. There were benches outside every house, which increased my yearning for a rest. We left the village and marched on an open plain. Although I thought that I was walking faster than before, I was actually falling behind. Suddenly, I realized that I was being overtaken by the last of our ranks.

'Los! Vorwaerts! (Get moving!)'

It was me the guard was shouting at. I turned around and saw him lifting his rifle. I quickly took a few steps forward, but it was too late. He had hit me in the back, and I collapsed. Once on the ground, I wanted to go to sleep.

I felt so comfortable, so nice and warm, that everything around me faded away; and, as at home, I pulled up my knees and closed my eyes. But then, as if I were someone else, I was walking again. Two men were holding my arms, preventing me from returning to the ground. They urged me to make an effort; they begged me to help them make me reach the camp, to try and use my legs. They told me that the guard would shoot me if I fell down again, but I didn't care. All I wanted was to sleep. Although I tried, I could not walk; because the moment they released their hold, my knees buckled as if they belonged to somebody else.

I must have fallen asleep while I was being dragged; because when we found ourselves suddenly outside the camp, my legs began working again. After being searched at the gate, I slowly walked the narrow path leading to the Entlausung. Once inside, I sat down on the bench in the 'undressing area'. While everyone else was undressing, I was trying to decide whether to go to sleep again.

At that moment, one of the attendants approached me and told me in Hebrew to go and hide behind the pile of discarded clothes and rest a bit. At first I did not recognize the man, but then the features became familiar. Eli Segal, my schoolmate who had introduced me to the Betar, was in charge of the 'undressing area'. The moment I recognized him I knew it was all right. I went behind the heap and fell asleep. Shortly before everybody was ready to go through showers, disinfection and the other formalities, Eli woke me up and rushed me through the showers, leading me to the end of the line.

Once outside, a Kapo took over and brought us to a hut where we joined some Jews from Poland. They told us that the Lithuanians were in the huts near the fence. The

111

hut we were in was only for people in transit. The next day they would probably put us in the huts for working brigades. Food was the same as in Lager Zehn. Only roll call was longer. On the night of our arrival, we were kept outside so long that more than four men collapsed. I held on, because having seen Eli in his clean uniform gave me hope that I too might get an easy job.

Next morning when they banged the hanging rail, I felt that I had only slept for a few minutes. The first day in Lager Eins passed with exercises. The Kapo was a Jew from Germany who made us march up and down the camp with intervals of 'caps down-caps up'. He especially had it in for the Jews from Poland, who, in his words, were Muselmaenner anyway, and every bit of food was wasted on them.

One of them, named Haim, who had arrived half-starved from the Lodz Ghetto a few weeks earlier, kept asking me questions during exercises. He was a real Muselmann. I had the feeling that I could simply lift him by the collar of his jacket. When it came to caps down, he always covered his head with his left hand. 'A Jew does not bare his head,' he told me in Yiddish. There were tiny crusts near his temples where they had torn off his peies. The barber in the Entlausung – a Jew – had done it. Haim told me that in 1939, the Germans had cut them off with scissors. He did not understand why the Jew in the Entlausung, who used a machine on everybody, had torn them off. He formed the distance of an inch between his fingers to show me how short they had been.

Why had the Jewish barber done it? What Haim and I did not know was that to many non-religious Jews, the observant one, clinging to his beard and peies, was the embodiment of calamity. It was because of him, the theory went, that the gentiles hated us. What to people like my father were the Ostjuden, to the secular Jews were the religious. It was they with their outlandish garb and their clannishness that brought on the persecutions. The secular Jew does not realize that his animosity is nothing but the revolt of the apostate against the Law – the Torah – of which every beard and peies-bearing Jew is a reminder. The visual appeal to his conscience arouses hatred and makes a Jew tear off the sidelocks of a fellow Jew. But in January 1945, all I could say was that I didn't know why the Jew in the Entlausung had torn off Haim's peies.

When I told him that my name was David, he sadly sighed 'Dovid Hamelekh' (King David), which he repeated to himself as if he remembered things which had happened years ago – perhaps in one of his dreams. It did not impress him that my father was a doctor. Haim only wanted to know if he put on tefillin; if I put on tefillin. And what about my mother. Did she keep kosher? Where was she?

Since leaving Stutthof, I had never asked myself the question. I had never asked anybody else. Now that Haim was looking at me and waiting for an answer as if I owed him one, I was at a loss. All I could see in my mind was her standing beyond the electrified barbed wire, throwing a piece of bread across. I told Haim that that was where she was – with my brother.

The next morning, he got near me again. 'You must say Kaddish right after "caps down-caps up,"' he whispered.

'What for?'

'They killed your mother and your brother.'

They had taken all the Lithuanian women and children

from Stutthof to Auschwitz. I felt nothing. Instead I rationalized. It was the thing to happen, the thing everybody knew would happen. Women and children who were useless, who could not work, had to be killed. My father told us once that Napoleon had killed the prisoners he had taken at Jaffa, when he could not feed them. It was the normal thing to do. It was even accepted in a way by many who put themselves in the Germans' shoes. What could they do with all those useless women and children? That question had entered my mind only late at night.

All of a sudden, I started to recall the method by which they had been killed. Everyone knew how it was done. Already in the Ghetto, two years earlier, the people talked about it. As I was trying to fall asleep, I pictured myself standing in front of the shed marked 'shower', getting inside, turning on the shower and receiving a whiff of gas from above instead of water. I was surprised, thinking at first that the water would follow. I turned the handle still more to the left in expectation. Then the sensation of choking – of trying to get back to the door, but being unable to because of everyone blocking the way. Did she try? Was my brother with her, or had they divided the men from the women? Maybe he was still alive. Maybe he had become a Kalfaktor (servant, spy), one of the young boys who had managed to get past selections and who were adopted by senior Kapos or Blockleiters (Block Leaders) to become their personal slaves, informers, and sometimes, sexual partners.

Today, it is still difficult for me to fall asleep, because I cannot get rid of the image of my mother in her last moments when she probably cried out to God – choking to death, because she had followed her husband.

114

It is enough if somebody mentions the 'Shoa' or if I walk past a bookstall and see titles like *The Holocaust* by Martin Gilbert for me to be unable to sleep and to ponder where those people got the impudence to alleviate – by generalization – the events which must be specified in order to explain their real significance. It was not part of any 'holocaust' to stand under the shower and expect water but be suffocated by gas. And for me to be unable to sleep, as I keep seeing myself there in my mother's place, is not unfathomable either. Kaddish is not enough.

THE RIGHTEOUS

We were loaded onto an open wagon drawn by a tractor and brought to Schwifting, a small village south of Landsberg. Nothing indicated that there was a war going on. As we were driven through the town, all the picture-postcard romance of German medieval townships returned to my mind. I recalled the character from Grimm's fairy tales, Frau Holle, shaking her eiderdown quilts, as I saw all the housewives airing their bedding in the clear winter morning and the horse-drawn platforms carting giant barrels of beer to their destination.

We were cold on the wagon, but we did not huddle together nor did we talk. We had been issued pickaxes and shovels but did not know where we were being taken. We feared that we might have to dig out people who had been shot, but for once we were actually let off where they had told us we would be.

If the wartime aspect of Landsberg was nothing but

peaceful, the village of Schwifting was like another world. Except for the two guards assigned to watch us, there was no uniform to be seen, no flag, no poster. The village church bell struck every quarter of an hour, but nobody walked on the streets and no vehicle passed throughout the day.

They let us off in teams of three, along the two-mile road of the village, to dig holes for telephone poles. The ground was frozen; and after a day's work, my hole partners and I had only picked loose about four inches of ground. The two guards patrolled from one end of the village to the other, crossing each other at twenty-minute intervals in the village centre near the spot where we were digging in front of a cottage opposite the church. One of our threesome, a youngster from Kovno who knew that I spoke German, suggested that I knock on one of the doors and ask for bread right after the guards had crossed each other. I knew it could be done. We did not dare to knock on the door next to our hole; because if the villager decided to denounce us, he would be able to point us out immediately. So the idea was to cross the road and try a few houses further down. The promises to share the bread assured me that neither of my partners would turn me in.

I crossed the road, reached a door, rang the bell, and became frightened. When the door was opened, I only could say one word – bread. I held out my hand like the beggars who used to come to our home, for whom small change was always ready on a small table near the door – put there by my mother and, at times, stolen by me. The German woman slammed the door in my face without a word – was that God's punishment? It was fortunate that my partners had observed me; otherwise they might have suspected me of eating the bread all by myself.

The following day when we had just arrived, the door facing our excavation opened and a small boy came out and quickly handed me three baked potatoes. I felt the warmth against my leg when I dropped them into my pocket; but at the same time, I remembered the acid taste of cooked potatoes I had eaten at the forge. For that reason alone, I immediately handed a potato to each partner. I ate the third one myself, hoping that the solidity of the crispy peel would prevent the taste of the potato from making me vomit.

For more than a week, the boy came out and gave me three potatoes. His name was Franz, and to this day, he keeps reminding me of the hypothetical ten righteous men in Sodom for whose sake Abraham haggled over its impending destruction (Genesis 18: 32).

In order to rid myself of that obligation to Franz the German, I returned to Schwifting in 1952 and brought him a silver chalice from Jerusalem to show my gratitude, to tear from my heart the feeling of debt towards an enemy. The German wasn't home, and I had to leave the chalice with his father. The effort was in vain. Until this day, I am haunted by the German boy and his potatoes; by the knowledge that he might have stood between me and death from hunger.

THE BLACK CAP

The Blockaeltester (Block Elder) of the privileged's dormitory was a Jew from Germany who had fled to Lithuania before the war and who had at one time been a patient of my father. I recognized him immediately. He used to visit us in the Ghetto. At the time, it had been rumoured that he was a spy for the Gestapo. Spy or not, I had to get to talk to him. There was no future in digging holes in frozen earth, while others were cleaning barracks, working in the kitchen, or sitting in offices. Although one was not allowed to go near the Priviligiertenblock (privileged's hut) where all those belonging to the camp staff were lodged, I took the risk one night and followed Mr Epstein after evening parade. I greeted him and asked him if he recognized me. He answered in the affirmative but added immediately that he had no food. I told him that I wasn't after food; but seeing that I was a locksmith, could he do the Germans a favour by recommending me to them. He promised to see what he could do, and a few days later they called my number at morning parade, instructing me to report to Oberscharfuehrer (Staff Sergeant) Tempel's office. He was in charge of administration.

After a short interrogation concerning my skills, he directed me to a small shed marked Schlosserei (Locksmith's Workshop) situated outside the main camp within the SS administration compound. My job was to maintain all the locks in the camp and the administrative compound and to do all repair jobs required by any of the SS personnel. After work, I was to report to the Priviligiertenblock, to the Blockaeltester. I spent the first day sorting tools and cleaning up. At night after roll-call, I returned to Mr Epstein in order to thank him. He showed me my space on the bunk which was near the door where all newcomers were placed. Then he congratulated me formally on my appointment to the post of Lagerschlosser, adding that I had made a very good impression on Oberscharfuehrer Tempel. The double bread ration I received proved that I had become a Priviligierter.

At roll-calls, we stood in formation at a right angle to the others, which gave me a feeling of superiority which was enhanced by the freedom to walk around the camp and outside the gate. The work was light, and the stove in the workshed created a feeling of cosy comfort amidst well-arranged tools and the smell of grease.

The fact that I spoke German brought all kinds of guards and low-ranking German personnel to my shed with requests for repairs on personal belongings – locks for suitcases, lockers, screeching doors. Someone even brought in a baby carriage for repair. It was his girlfriend's he told me – a woman whose husband was at the front. I was often given bread, sausages and cigarettes for doing these repairs. Since I did not smoke, I exchanged the cigarettes for bread and margarine.

As the weeks passed, I was able to afford the black cap, the status symbol every Priviligierter wore as a sign of his emancipation. I ordered the cap from the Lagerschneider (camp tailor) to whom I paid four cigarettes and one bread ration. Forgotten were the days of hunger. The flannel-lined headgear, styled exactly as the black high-peaked SS winter cap, except for the skull and crossbones, provided a sense of power and a feeling of contempt towards all those who did not belong to this upper caste of privileged servants to the Germans. Wearing the non-regulation headgear was not only tolerated by the camp authorities, it was encouraged. I was also entitled to a black armband with a white inscription, 'Lagerschlosser'; but due to wartime shortages, I had to do without. Nevertheless, the cap was enough of a distinction. It had to be drawn and slapped against the thigh whenever one met a German, but it made the others move out of our way. They were scared of those of us who wore the black caps.

One day, my father marched into the camp, in transit within the ranks of a column of prisoners. He called my name. At first, I did not recognize the Muselmann who was shouting, but then I did in spite of the broken voice and fleshless face. He was no longer my father. He looked straight at my black cap and begged me for some bread, but I turned away.

Because I would have let him die of hunger – because I wished he had died of hunger – I used to answer questions about him for many years by saying that he died of hunger. But he didn't. He was transferred to Labour Camp Four and became a Kapo helping to evacuate the camp in the last days of the war. The train which took the survivors of the camp to the south was strafed by allied planes and he, together with his guards and other prisoners, was killed. Some survived, and one of them told me the story.

PESSAH

Spring 1945 was very cold. The sky was crystal clear, but the ground was frozen. The prisoners shivered in their tattered uniforms as they shuffled back and forth from camp to site, trying to warm their hands under their armpits. Some were courageous enough to risk being caught walking away from their jobs at the SS camp to seek some warmth at the stove I always had going in the workshop. The sign I had ordered from the camp painter, 'Unbefugten ist der Eintritt strengstens verboten! (Unauthorized entry strictly forbidden) made a good impression on Oberscharfuehrer Tempel, but the prisoners probably didn't understand the 'Unbefugten'. No matter how much I shouted, no matter how much I threatened, either a gardener or a latrine worker would suddenly enter the workshop without knocking and go for the stove with outstretched hands.

'Raus du Schweinehund!' I would shout, raising a hammer or any other handy tool and chase them out, kicking their behinds for emphasis.

Since the day Tempel had seen me at it and had smiled, I always hoped he would hear me shout and smile at me again. Mr Epstein, too, was very proud of me. When I brought him half a packet of cigarettes I had been given for making a reserve magazine for Tempel's gun, he told me to keep it. The satisfaction of a job well done – the bullets fitted smoothly into the magazine which snapped into the gun as if it had been factory made. To receive cigarettes from the most feared man in the camp gave me such a feeling of well-being that I no longer cared whether the war would end. I had enough to eat; the Muselmaenner feared me; the Oberscharfuehrer trusted me with his gun and bullets. Maybe as more prisoners arrived, I would be able to extend the workshop and get an assistant or two.

As I was musing about the future, warming my hands above the stove, the door opened with a gust of cold air. Another Muselmann came in.

'Raus!' I shouted, but the man came closer.

'Reb Dovid,' he said, and I suddenly felt as if the ground was giving way under me. The Yiddish words – my name spoken with the respectful title indicating an intimate friendliness – tugged at me with a force I could not withstand. I looked at the eyes burning in the skin-covered skull and realized that it was Haim.

'Raus!' I tried again, but there was no strength, no conviction any more in my German superiority. There was no more feeling of might. As Haim held out his cupped hand to me. I noticed that he had a small heap of white powder.

'What do you want?' I asked him.

'I want to bake a Matze (unleavened bread). Here, I brought some flour.'

'A Matze?!' I exclaimed. 'Are you crazy?'

'Reb Dovid, don't you know that it is Pessah (Passover)?'

I gave him water, and he mixed the flour. He put the tiny bit of paste on the stove; and when it was dry, he lifted it off with his spoon. He took my arm and asked me to say the blessing with him. I did not do it. I flew into a rage.

'Raus!' I shouted again, and he left without a word.

Today when I want to say the words on Passover, I must fight my tears; because I remember my mother, who was beaten by my father just before the Kiddush, and Haim who appears before me every Seder night, asking me to say the blessing. It reminds me of how much I had been like my father, and how, by chasing Haim away, I may have ceased to be a Jew.

I have come to the conclusion that only if one considers himself his brother's keeper as Haim did – only if one abides by the dictum that '[the children of] Israel are guarantors to each other' (*Babylonian Talmud*, Tract. Shvuot, 39: 1) is there a chance of survival for the Jewish people as a nation, for Judaism as an idea, a way of life, with the Law, where death is death and where crimes are crimes – and not a 'holocaust'.

THE INTELLECTUAL LOCKSMITH

The Germans have a proverb which says that if the ass has it too good, he goes dancing on the ice. So when I, Haeftling (prisoner) number 91892, the 'Lagerschlosser', was no longer hungry, I forgot myself.

I was called to the SS library to repair a door and noticed a pile of books not yet arranged on the shelves. Thinking that the time had come for a little entertainment, I chose the pocket edition of *Hermann und Dorothea* by Wolfgang von Goethe. I hid it under my jacket and left the library. I had not taken ten steps when the librarian came after me and demanded that I return the stolen book. I had miscalculated. Having exchanged a few words with the librarian, an SS Rottenfuehrer (Corporal) who showed a friendly disposition towards me – the German-speaking locksmith – I did not realize that my speaking German would arouse the SS man's suspicion and make him check the pile of books immediately after I left. Having allowed me to work alone in the room, the librarian had wanted to test my honesty. Eventually this dawned on me. I took out the book and handed it back. I started to beg, fearing that I would lose my job as Lagerschlosser, but the German took me by the collar and dragged me to Tempel's office.

'If you had asked for it, I would have lent it to you; but since you are a thief, you must be punished.'

Oberscharfuehrer Tempel did not raise his voice. He simply ordered me to lie down on the whipping bench. I counted every lash I received on my behind. After fifteen lashes, Tempel let me get up.

'Danke, Herr Oberscharfuehrer,' I muttered according

to regulation and slapped my cap on my thigh fearing that I would collapse. A slap in the face brought me back to my senses. Tempel marched me to the gate and commanded me to stand at the right post. As soon as the columns started marching in, I had to repeat: 'Ich stehle keine Buecher mehr (I shall not steal books again).' Tempel, who was checking the returning columns, saw to it that I kept it up, loud and clear, without interruption. I was the laughing stock of the Privilegiertenblock, but I was not dismissed. My love for the German classics had probably caused the librarian to put in a good word for me. But similar to the distaste I had acquired for potatoes, I never touched a German classic again. I still wonder though what *Hermann und Dorothea* is about.

FREEDOM

ROOSEVELT

'Roosevelt is dead!'

It was April 12, 1945. The news ran through the camp almost as rapidly as the rumour had spread about the attempt on Hitler's life a year earlier. For the coming weeks, the prisoners watched the daily formations of American bombers pass in the clear sky above, flying to the east to bomb Munich. Thin aluminium strips fell like silver rain, arousing everybody's curiosity. During the night artillery fire could be heard in the distance. Everyone knew that the Americans were approaching. Everyone regained hope that he would survive, except for the Muselmaenner who continued shuffling back and forth to work, collapsing during roll-calls, and begging for bread.

I was surprised at the alarm and the mood of mourning which spread through the camp at the news that Roosevelt was dead. The Germans rejoiced. An enemy without a leader, even if only temporarily, meant respite for them. Yet I could not understand why the Jews should be saddened by the death of a gentile, or by the death of anybody for that matter, after having lost most of their relatives; although I could understand their apprehension that the death of the American President might cause the war to be extended. The forebodings seemed to have been justified, because life in Lager Eins continued as usual. The death of Roosevelt turned out to be just an emotional interlude.

LIBERATION

The SS man asked for a screwdriver. I gave it to him, and he went outside to scrape the 'SS' off the license plate of his motorcycle. He handed back the tool, thanked me, hopped on his machine and roared off.

The Americans were only forty miles away.

I thought of escape, but rejected it because of the warmth and cosiness provided by my stove. Nevertheless, I took a pair of pliers with me in case I might have to cut through the fence in an emergency. There was no plan, no purpose in my mind. There was no hope for anything; just an element of fear, because I knew that if the Germans left, they would take us with them or kill us.

There were fewer guards and some towers remained unmanned.

One morning, we were ordered not to leave the camp. All the privileged were to stay inside. Everyone had to pass selection for the march to Dachau. The camp was to be evacuated within 48 hours. Listening to Tempel announce the evacuation of Lager Eins, I decided that no matter what happened, I would not go on any more marches. The last time two prisoners had helped me when I could no longer walk, but this time they would just leave me to be shot if I fell behind. The black cap would be of no use during evacuation, the same way as the doctor's pouch had not been of any use to my father when we arrived at Stutthof.

126

No. I was going to do anything in order not to leave. If they wanted to shoot me, let them do it where I was. There was no need for me to walk miles and miles only to be shot a day or two later.

I walked up to Dr Greenberg, a colleague of my father, and asked him to let me stay. He advised against it, but then gave in to my entreaties and sent me back into the camp. The next morning, I did not go to the Appellplatz. The Privilegiertenblock was empty. I got into the far end and hid under Mr Epstein's straw.

In the afternoon, Tempel opened the door. He shouted, 'Alles raus!', fired two shots, but did not search the hut. He went away, leaving the door wide open. For hours, I waited under the straw and watched the entrance, trying to guess from which direction the sounds of single pistol shots were coming. The rumble of heavy artillery grew heavier and, as it became dark, lightning preceded every explosion.

It was not until late in the night that I finally ventured outside. I crawled towards the fence and tried to cut the wire with the pliers, because I assumed that the barbed wire was no longer electrified since there were no lights on in the camp. A burst of machine-gun fire from nearby scared me, and I crawled back to the hut to hide again. There was more machine-gun fire at dawn. Then, as it became completely light, everything was quiet.

I stepped outside and saw a commotion near the kitchen. Tens of prisoners were trying to get inside through the windows. Having been without food and water for more than twenty-four hours, I joined the fray. I dealt blows right and left and pushed ahead to reach the window until I finally got into the kitchen. Everyone inside was eating. I found a loaf of bread and fought my way to another window to get outside again; but as I climbed onto the sill to jump outside, someone pulled the loaf from under my arm and ran. I was too exhausted to pursue him.

In the *mêlée*, I had lost my black cap. Feeling very cold and insecure without it, I went back to the Privilegiertenblock for my old striped prisoner's cap, the one they had given me at Stutthof. I pulled it all the way down over my ears and went outside again. There was a faucet near the Schreibstube (camp office). I tried it but there was no water. I noticed that the gate stood partially open, and I looked up at the watch-towers. The glass-covered cabins seemed empty. I turned towards the gate, but the sudden fear of a hidden machine gun or Tempel appearing with a gun made me return to my block where I stayed hidden for another night. I felt nothing else but the gnawing in my stomach, the dryness in my throat, and the sound of artillery in my ears. Then a machine-gun went off nearby.

The ground was strewn with bodies. Unaware of a guard who had remained on a tower, some had been mowed down while trying to open the gate, others when climbing over it. When I finally gathered the courage to try and reach it myself, I had to step on heads and limbs. Suddenly a hand clutched at my ankle and a raucous voice pleaded:

'Ich vil aich zain frai! (I too want to be free!)'

I bent back the anonymous fingers, one by one, almost breaking them, and shouted back into the heap, 'Du bist toit! (You are dead!)'

I pushed myself through the narrow opening. Once outside, I went straight to the SS kitchen. The place was crowded with prisoners. Everyone was eating. I grabbed a loaf of bread, a packet of margarine, and a bowl full of marmalade. There was an officer's jacket hanging on a nail near the window. Somebody had torn off the insignia and shoulder tabs, but it was still a good jacket. I put it on – it was a perfect fit. I buttoned all the metal buttons, including the ones on the pockets, and went outside towards the road. I was exhausted and sat down on the grass to eat my bread and my marmalade, but in the rush had forgotten the margarine on the windowsill where I had found the jacket. I was too tired to go back for it.

The screech of chains and the noise of heavy motors came nearer. Two tanks roared past with white five-pointed stars painted on the side – just like the Russians I remembered, only white instead of red. Another two, and then I stopped counting them as they rolled on towards the town. I finished the marmalade. The bread was hard, but I kept at it bit by bit using the pliers to break off pieces.

Then they came. Hands above their heads. German soldiers, officers, OT men – all in uniform – marching towards the camp in close formation, guarded by black American soldiers chewing something. As they marched past, I noticed Oberscharfuehrer Tempel among them. He too was without insignia, without shoulder tabs and without his cap on which he wore his second face – the skull and crossbones.

It was then that sadness fell upon me. I felt that I had been one of them, that I should be marching at their side, that 'we' had lost the war to Negroes who by now were throwing chocolate bars at me, which I ate after the prisoners of war disappeared beyond the camp. I waved at Tempel, wondering if he had seen me – hoping that he had.

On the day of liberation, it was not a Jew sitting outside the concentration camp, but a deformed German –

a would-have-been SS man without a personality – a crippled soul.

Even now, half a century later, in spite of wife, of children and of children's children, I still see myself sitting on the ground. wearing a German officer's coat, a Jewish prisoner's cap and trousers, wondering who I am, asking myself when, if ever, I shall be free.

MARRIAGE

And Isaac brought her into his mother Sarah's tent, and took Rebecca, and she became his wife; and he loved her. And Isaac was comforted after his mother's death.

(Genesis, 24: 67)

As Rebecca was chosen for Isaac, so my wife was chosen for me by my mother. For when I first saw her, a voice within me told me that this was the woman my mother would have wanted me to marry. And as Isaac had done before me. I took her into my mother's spiritual tent and was comforted after my mother's death.

But comfort was not enough. I placed her between myself and the outside world which I knew had not changed. It took the better part of thirty years until I could start to face myself within that world where, concealed behind a mask of decency provided by full stomachs, the Kapos, the policemen and the Oberjuden (Super(vising) Jews) continue their dance of life. Their lives, like 'a poor player that struts and frets his hour upon the stage . . . full of sound and fury, signifying nothing'.[26]

Continuing my life amongst them, behind the shield of my wife's devotion, I searched the abyss of my experience for something to counter the Macbethian philosophy. It was provided by my youngest daughter when she interrogated me – when she forced me to try and turn the non-significance into a thing of value.

Encouraged by her understanding, I started lecturing; telling the young people how it really was; how, unless we adopt a set of rules by which to live, we will soon start howling like the wolves, eventually becoming one of them.

AFTERWORD

THE COVENANT

The yeshiva (Talmudical college) outside Ashdod wanted me to stay for Shabbat (the Sabbath) to talk to the students. The parasha (Biblical portion) to be read that Shabbat was Noah. Anxious to reach the yeshiva before sunset, I rushed to the Central Bus Station in the shadow of gathering clouds. I took my seat in the bus just as rain started pouring down. All the way to Ashdod the water streamed down outside the windows, and I was worried how I would be able to cover the quarter of a mile from the bus stop to the yeshiva on foot without being drenched. Waiting for the rain to stop was out of the question. I was invited for Shabbat, and I could not be late. However, as I stepped off the bus, the rain suddenly stopped; and as I entered the path leading to the yeshiva, I saw a rainbow whose arc was like a fiery gate on the black horizon.

Parashat Noah! I remembered.

And it shall come to pass, when I bring a cloud over the earth, that the bow shall be seen in the cloud.

And I will remember my covenant, which is between me and you and every living creature of all flesh; and the waters shall no more become a flood to destroy all flesh.'

(Genesis, 9: 14–15)

But what if He, the Almighty, changed his mind? The sins of the generation of the deluge were trifles in comparison with those committed by Jews in modern Israel. The list would read like whole chapters out of Jeremiah. However, in my mind, the biggest crime of all was the complacency of our people while Jews were being killed again.

'TAL MOSES PASSED AWAY' screamed the headline on July 6, 1987 in *Hadashot*, an Israeli newspaper:

> He was five and a half when he died. He was fatally burnt when a petrol bomb was thrown at the family car at the Habla intersection near Kalkilya. His mother, Ofrah Moses, was killed in the attack, today is his funeral.

The newspaper report, one among many similar ones, using the words 'passed away' and 'died' instead of 'was murdered' was covering up a tragedy as deep as the one of Jews being led to their deaths in Europe.

But my thoughts went back to my mother. Wasn't Ofrah Moses like her – both trapped and both choked to death? My mother stood under the shower suffocating with her child clinging to her, and was then incinerated. Ofrah Moses cried out in agony suffocating with her son Tal, and then burned to death.

And Jewish judges hold that 'their only sin was being Jewish'.

Looking at the rainbow, I feared that God might change His mind. Because the deaths of Jewish women and children had gone unpunished – and even unmourned – He might revoke His covenant.

My mood was gloomy. We recited the blessing after the

meal, and I immediately started my lecture as they were still carting away the dishes and leftover food – the half-eaten loaves of bread to be thrown away – and I told them how in the Ghetto we used to run a lottery for the hardest slice of bread. They asked questions for hours.

The next morning when they honoured me with the aliya (being called up to the reading of the Torah in the synagogue), I refused.

'But why?' one of the younger ones implored, tugging at my tallis.

'Because I am not worthy.'

He called his rabbi, who came and told me, 'Come Reb Dovid,' calling me as Haim had done before him, 'all Jews are worthy.'

I read out the blessing and followed the parasha, still fearing that the covenant with Noah might be revoked because of our unworthiness.

When one considers the effort most primitive societies make to structure social systems and moral codes, one wonders how the Jewish people destined to be a 'nation of priests and holy men' (Exodus 19: 6) so easily abandoned their call and their obligations – those undertaken by their forefathers and carried on by following generations at tremendous sacrifice.

Bewailing the fate of those Jews who perished throughout the centuries, one must not lose sight of the interrelationship between their abandonment of Jewish values and the consequent disasters which befell them. It is beyond the scope of this book to describe the constantly recurring relinquishment of trust in the uniqueness of spiritual resurrection in the light of the universally prevalent Macbethian concept of life, i.e. that life is 'signifying nothing', one cannot help but speak of a miracle in its profoundest sense.

When I refer to Jews and their values, I do not mean the bagel-and-lox heroes of a Philip Roth or the intellectual hypochondriacs of a Saul Bellow. Nor do I accept expressions such as 'the values of the Judeo-Christian civilization', so dear to Jewish intellectuals who are strangers in a world which has made no progress since the days of Abraham, except in the field of technology.

To view civilization in the context of the concentration camp, or to remember that a thirty years' war was fought between two conflicting Christian doctrines in order to establish supremacy of ownership over various parts of Europe, and then to speak of civilization based on a Judeo-Christian philosophy is nothing but a hypocritical invention by those who have lost their own values and are unable to accept those of others.

No amount of 'cheek-turning' will secure for a Jew his place in 'modern society'. Yet by unequivocally clinging to his heritage, he may still emerge as 'a light unto the nations' (Isaiah 42: 6).

There are, of course, 'Judeo-Christian' aspirations, but they do not seem to reach beyond the dreams inspired by the wares displayed at Bloomingdale's or by the New York Stock Exchange of which the State of Israel has become a branch. Both the material and spiritual aspirations in the great Jewish centres in the United States and Israel carry the germs of physical and spiritual destruction.

There are two ways one can foresee disaster: one is by realizing that assimilation into gentile societies will provoke strong rejection, or by taking the warning of the Bible literally:

And the Lord said unto Moses: Behold thou shalt sleep with thy fathers; and this people will rise up and go whoring after the gods of the strangers of the land, whither they go to be among them, and will forsake me, and break my covenant which I have made with them. Then my anger shall be kindled against them in that day, and I will forsake them, and I will hide my face from them, and they shall be devoured, and many evils and troubles shall befall them; so that they will say in that day: Are not these evils come upon us, because our God is not among us?

(Deuteronomy, 31: 16–17)

Anti-semitism, the scapegoat for almost any economic, social, political or religious failure, is nothing but the rejection of the Jew as a supposed watchman of the conscience of humanity. The absence of abnegation, of modesty, and the lack of intellectual integrity which, first and foremost, imposes upon the Jew the acceptance and observance of the Law, makes him appear as a hypocrite, especially in the eyes of those to whom the commandment of 'thou shalt not kill' is something negotiable, something to be believed in by 'free choice' or to be rejected if contrary to vested interest.

The Jewish State, built with the hopes of those to whom the Jewishness of the state was the essential motive of their sacrifices, may well find itself going down the path towards its own destruction. If the 'Judeo-Christian' civilization submerges its 'Judeo' part by letting it wither in its mildewy cellar of perfunctory religious ceremonies, while the secular part disintegrates through drugs, corruption, and collaboration with the enemy.[27]

Assimilation by a whole nation and the search for a faith

in a superior god, easily personified by a superior gentile, brings forth the worst. Just as those who collaborated with the Germans by endeavouring first to be like them, then to be liked by them, then to identify with them, eventually became temporary masters by permission of the members of the 'master race', so too the Jewish leaders of today seek to emulate their foreign providers of cultural and worldly goods and gods.

The substitution of the responsibility of each Jew for his fellow Jew – by liberalism and secular humanism, frees everyone of almost every social obligation other than the payment of taxes. It is another form of assimilation into a world where only the production, consumption and the acquisition of goods are accepted social virtues.

This type of assimilation, manifested by the secularization of Jewish education in Israel and in the rest of the world – and not differing much from the one that I received in Austria or in Lithuania – will eventually destroy every Jewish feeling of belonging and lead to the disintegration of the fabric holding Jewish communities together under alien pressure. It is aided and abetted by Jewish leaders whose greed is matched only by their lust for power and honour – real or imaginary.

When I came to Israel in 1948, I was quite surprised to find that the need of many Jews for father figures and for 'fatherlands' had not lost any of its strength. Having abandoned religion as the 'opium of the people', they hung Stalin's portraits in the dining rooms of their kibbutzim (collective agricultural settlements), calling him the 'father of the nations', 'the sun of the working class'. The Soviet Union was termed 'the Second Fatherland', the 'spiritual' one, with Jossip Vissarionovich (Djugashvili) Stalin their father.

Fatherlands, portraits on the wall, and flags – all 'sound and fury' – continued to follow me around the world; but none was able to rally me to its cause.

Once, carried away by my own rhetoric during one of my lectures a few years ago, I made a statement which on the face of it seemed devoid of logic. However, having made it intuitively, I did not filter it through the sieve of intellectual deliberation. I was referring to an accident in which two cars collided on a Saturday at an intersection, both drivers having disregarded the traffic light. I said that whoever does not observe the Shabbat does not observe anything at all. What I wished to convey was that a man must accept a set of rules; and as the observance of the Shabbat is the most important pillar of the Jewish ethic (Maimonides wrote in his Mishne Torah that 'Shabbat and idolatry . . . both outweigh all the rest of the Torah's commandments'), its non-observance by a Jew will deprive him of the very basis for observing any law or regulation. It will 'free' him of all obligations.

The traffic light was only an illustration for the deeper meaning of the non-observance of Shabbat. The total disregard of moral precepts by Jewish leaders and individuals made it impossible for them to accept the rule laid down by Maimonides: 'And if idolators said, "Give us one of you and we shall kill him, if not we shall kill all of you," all shall be killed, not delivering one soul of Israel.'[28] They not only handed over individual Jews, but whole trainloads to be slaughtered in order to save themselves and their relatives.

A striking example of such actions emerged from the judgment handed down on June 22, 1955 at the District Court of Jerusalem, by Dr B. Halevy:

. . . with the active assistance by Jews like Dr Belesz and Kohani, calming mendacious announcements were disseminated by the Nazi and Hungarian authorities, in the name of the Jewish Council – and 18,000 of the deceived victims of Eichmann, Crumey and Wislizeny boarded the trains, transport after transport, to be carried to the gas chambers of Auschwitz. Only on June 9, 1944, after the Kluj Ghetto was emptied of all its inhabitants, the signal was given to the SS to transfer the leaders of the community, the relatives of Dr Kastner, including Belesz and Kohani, with some tens of baptized Jews, protégés of Urban and the head of the Gestapo, altogether a total of 388 souls rescued from Kluj, to the camp of the privileged in Budapest.[29]

The non-Jewish concept that confession automatically leads to absolution has been adopted by most post-destruction Jews who, by absolving pity-arousing biographical historians, find justification and absolution for their own complicity or apathy.

Two members of the Kovno Aeltestenrat – Leib Garfunkel and Abraham Tory who survived to publish their memoirs – give almost matching accounts of the activities of Serebrowicz and Lipcer, the Gestapo representatives. (See pp. 56, 64.)

Both chroniclers attempt to disassociate themselves from those men who, in many instances, were called upon to act at the behest of the Aeltestenrat, and were part and parcel of the Ghetto administration. Although not appointed by it, they fit neatly into the framework of favouritism and corruption which was the hallmark of every power structure erected by the Germans.

Garfunkel describes how:

... as time went on, the border line dividing egoistic reasoning and public reasoning became distorted and in many instances almost disappeared ... This 'Ghettosophy' (the acquiescence) arose undoubtedly from the egoistic feeling of each individual, who above all searched for a way to save himself and the members of his family. It was natural that everyone looked upon his personal fate and on the future of the ghetto from his personal point of view.[30]

This example is enough to dismiss the mental acrobatic hoops through which apologetic historiographers – especially in Israel – wish to propel their readers in order to justify a bankrupt leadership.

Abraham Tory stated in retrospect that

at the beginning of the war [in Lithuania 1941] we feared what was in store for men, if they fell into the hands of the Germans, but it crossed nobody's mind that they would murder women, children and the old.[31]

This is nothing but an attempt at whitewashing, supported by the academic sycophants of Israel's establishment, considering that German atrocities perpetrated in Poland on men, women, children and the old since September 1939 were already widely known. His 'nobody' is the arrogant invention of a self-appointed leader who, by feigning ignorance and imputing it to others, seeks to vindicate himself by making them responsible for public actions determined by the needs of his own personal safety and survival. It is a posthumous insult to those who knew, who warned, who were silenced and were wilfully ignored.

A most striking piece of falsification is a document (see pp. 144–5) produced by Tory showing the draft of the proclamation issued by the Aeltestenrat on October 27, 1941 calling upon the Ghetto population to assemble the next morning, knowing that ten thousand of the assembled would be taken away and killed by the Germans. The chronicler describes the erasures and corrections appearing on the facsimile as 'showing the serious scruples of the Jews' Council' while anybody familiar with the German language will realize that all the 'scruples' were of a grammatical nature, in the endeavour to turn out a document in perfect German, to please and to impress the originators of the concentration order.[32]

I too was part of that administrative system – or at least my father was and thus my survival may be largely attributed to it. But today, when I attempt to shed some light on the obfuscation created by similar survivors by offering my own experiences as a counterweight to their misconstructions, it is my duty to point to those events where leaders and those that they led reacted differently to secure both their physical and spiritual survival. The most noteworthy instance is the active participation of the members of the Lachwa Ghetto council in armed resistance, thereby allowing six hundred Jews to escape after two thousand had actively resisted deportation in September 1942.[33]

It is relatively easy to try and reach conclusions in social, national, or political contexts. Following one's inclinations and using systematic research, scientifically valid results can be reached. It is much harder to formulate the personal consequences derived from past events. The problem stems from the fact that these consequences depend to a large extent on the pressures of daily needs and do not

141

become a permanent set of rules determining future actions or behaviour.

I shall, nevertheless, endeavour in these concluding lines to separate the frustrated SS man from the incomplete Jew – to salvage that which still may be of value.

When I was asked during one of my lectures which of my experiences was the worst, I had to choose between my father taking off my yarmulke – dethroning God – and his dragging me to be handed over to the Germans. Speaking in front of students aged sixteen to eighteen – wishing to convey the truth and to show the depth of the tragedy which could be repeated and not just to satisfy idle curiosity – the choice could not be intellectual but had to be emotional. Writing for an adult audience, I could have cited extensively from memoirs and works of history in an attempt to rationalize and provide valid scientific explanations; but quotations cannot heal the open wound which starts to bleed inside me whenever I hear or say the words, Boruch Ato . . . (Blessed art Thou . . .).

As much as the SS man might try to escape by wresting tears of pity from Jews with stories of cruelty and mayhem, as much as he might seek exoneration by means of learned dissertations, there is always Haim to remind him that it is the observance of the Law which gives the life of a Jew meaning and direction. His offering of the Matze in order to prevent my fall, his assuming my guarantorship under the rule by which all Jews are bound, may well be the reason why I am still alive.

It is Friday afternoon. I shall soon put away my pen, and the candles will be lit. Later, grandchildren, daughters and sons-in-law will come, stand there, bare-headed, politely

142

listening in discomfort to the Kiddush, watching me like an anachronism as I bless the wine, the bread – and then as always at this point, Haim will return to my mind and urge me:

'Reb Dovid, teach them, warn them, tell them that it was no "holocaust"!'

Meldung

Der Aeltestenrat wurde von den Machtorganen aufgefordert, der Ghettobevölkerung mitzuteilen folgenden Befehl der Machtorgane mitzuteilen:

Sämtliche Ghettoeinwohner, ohne irgendwelche Ausnahme, darunter auch Kinder und Kranke, sind verpflichtet, am Dienstag, den 28. Oktober 1941, nicht später als 6 Uhr früh, ihre Wohnungen zu verlassen und sich auf dem Platze, zwischen den grossen Blocks und der Demokratu Strasse befindet, zu versammeln und sich laut Anordnung der Polizei aufzustellen.

Die Ghettoeinwohner müssen sich in Familien aufstellen, das arbeitende Familienhaupt mit einen Familienangehörigen,

Die Wohnungen, Schränke, Büfetts, Tische usw. nicht verschlossen bleiben.

Nach 6 Uhr morgens darf niemand in den Wohnungen bleiben. Diejenigen, die sich nach 6 Uhr früh werden, auf der Stelle erschossen.

Wianuoli, den 27 Oktober 1941.

המקור, המעיד על הלבטים הקשים של מועצת היהודים, אצל בעל היומן

ANNOUNCEMENT

The Council of Elders was ordered by the authorities to notify the Ghetto population of the following order of the authorities: [**Correction**: *verb crossed out and moved to end of sentence according to German grammatical rule*.]

All Ghetto residents without exception whatsoever, including children and sick, are obliged, on Tuesday the 28th October 1941 not later than 6 o'clock in the morning, to leave their homes and to assemble at the square between the great blocks and Demokratu Street and to position themselves in accordance with orders of the [*Jewish*] police. [**Correction**: *'arrange themselves' substituted by 'position themselves'*.]

The Ghetto residents must draw themselves up in families with the working head of family in front. [**Correction**: *'familywise' substituted by 'in families'. Crossed out: 'together with the members of his family who are being maintained by him'*.]

The homes, cupboards, side-boards, tables etc., are not allowed to be locked. [**Crossed out**: *'must not remain locked'*.]

After 6 o'clock in the morning nobody is allowed to stay in the homes. Those who who will be found in their homes after 6 o'clock in the morning, will be shot on the spot. [**Crossed out**: *'Transgressors will be shot at once'*.]

Viliampole, the 27th October 1941.

Diary Editor's note in Hebrew): '*The original, showing the "heavy scruples" of the Jewish Council, is in possession of the owner of the diary.*'

(Translation of document, opposite)

FOOTNOTES AND BIBLIOGRAPHY

1. *Yediot Aharonot*, daily newspaper (Tel–Aviv, July 11, 1989).
2. *Time International* (New York, March 18, 1985).
3. Laws of Israel:

    a. Law for bringing Nazis and their helpers to justice, 1950.

    b. Law of the remembrance of the *Shoa* and the heroism – Yad va'Shem, 1953.

    c. Law for the prohibition of the denial of the *Shoa*, 1986.
4. Gilbert, Martin. *Atlas of the Holocaust* (Rainbow Publishing Group Ltd, London, 1982) title page.
5. Trunk, Isaiah: *Judenrat, The Jewish Councils in Eastern Europe under Nazi Occupation* (Stein and Day, New York, 1977) title page; *Jewish Responses to Nazi Persecution* (Stein and Day, New York, 1982) title page.
6. Arendt, Hanna, *Eichmann in Jerusalem* (Viking, New York, 1963).
7. Hilberg, Raul, *The Destruction of the European Jews* (Holmes & Meier Publishers, Inc., New York, 1985), p. 293.
8. Arendt, *op. cit.*, p. 104.
9. Garfunkel, Leib, *The Destruction of Kovno's Jewry* (Yad va'Shem, Jerusalem, 1963), p. 54. (Garfunkel was a member of the Kovno Ghetto *Aeltestenrat*.)
10. The subject of Jewish names (p. 10) is treated in detail in Karl, Emil Franzos, *Halb-Asien, Band 6, Aus*

der grossen Ebene, Namenstudien (Stuttgart: Cotta'sche Buchhandlung, 1897).

11. Reitlinger, Gerald, *The Final Solution* (Sphere Books Ltd, London, 1971), p. 16.

12. Jabotinsky, Zeev, *Complete Works, Baderech La'Medina*, (Eri Jabotinsky Publishers, Jerusalem, 1953), p. 308.

13. Hecht, Ben, *A Child of the Century* (Simon & Schuster, New York, 1954), p. 531.

14. *Hadashot*, daily newspaper (Tel–Aviv, November 3, 1989).

15. Reitlinger, *op. cit.*, p. 9.

16. Grilak, Menahem, *Ot Cain* (Herzliya, 1989), pp. 259–61.

17. Arendt, *op. cit.*, pp. 105–6.

18. Tory, Avraham, *Ghetto Everyday* (Bialik Institute and Tel-Aviv University, Tel-Aviv, 1988), p. 353. (Tory was General Secretary and member of the Kovno Ghetto *Aeltestenrat*.)

19. *Ibid.*, p. 68.

20. *Ibid.*, p. 237.

21. *Yediot Aharonot*, daily newspaper (Tel-Aviv, July 11, 1989).

22. Garfunkel, *op. cit.*, p. 183.

23. *Ibid.*, p. 171.

24. Levi, Primo, *The Drowned and the Saved* (New York: Summit Books, 1988), pp. 83–4.

25. Bat-Zvi, Pnina, morning broadcast on *Galei Zahal*, the Israel Defense Forces Radio Broadcasting Service, December 25, 1987.

26. Shakespeare, William, *Macbeth*, Act V, Scene v, lines 24–8, (Oxford University Press, London 1943).

27. Weizmann, Ezer, Israel Minister of Science, quoted in *Yediot Aharonot*, January 2, 1990 following the disclosure by Israel's Prime Minister, Yitzhak Shamir, of Weizmann's secret illegal talks with the Palestine Liberation Organization (PLO): 'I guided the PLO to say exactly what Shimon Peres [Deputy Prime Minister] told me to.'

28. Rabbi Moshe Ben-Maimon (Maimonides), *Mishne Torah* (*The Book of Knowledge*), (Mossad Harav Kook, Jerusalem, 1985) p. 7.

29. Rosenfeld, Shalom, *Tik Plili 124*, (Karni Publishers Ltd, Tel-Aviv, 1955), p. 419.

30. Garfunkel, *op. cit.*, pp. 261–2.

31. Tory, *op. cit.*, p. 28.

32. *Ibid.*, p. 64 (comment by Dina Porat, scientific editor).

33. Trunk, *op. cit.*, pp. 471–2.

The quotations on pages v and 91 are from Primo Levi, *The Drowned and the Saved* (New York: Summit Books, 1988), pp. 82–4.